Programming Reactive Extensions and LINQ

Jesse Liberty
Paul Betts

Apress®

Programming Reactive Extensions and LINQ

ISBN-13 (pbk): 978-1-4302-3747-1

ISBN-13 (electronic): 978-1-4302-3748-8

President and Publisher: Paul Manning
Lead Editor: Ewan Buckingham
Technical Reviewer: Stefan Turalski
Editorial Board: Steve Anglin, Mark Beckner, Ewan Buckingham, Gary Cornell, Morgan Engel,
    Jonathan Gennick, Jonathan Hassell, Robert Hutchinson, Michelle Lowman, James Markham,
    Matthew Moodie, Jeff Olson, Jeffrey Pepper, Douglas Pundick, Ben Renow-Clarke,
    Dominic Shakeshaft, Gwenan Spearing, Matt Wade, Tom Welsh
Coordinating Editor: Jessica Belanger
Copy Editor: Kimberly Burton
Indexer: BIM Indexing & Proofreading Services
Production Support: Patrick Cunningham
Cover Designer: Anna Ishchenko

Distributed to the book trade worldwide by Springer Science+Business Media, LLC., 233 Spring Street, 6th Floor, New York, NY 10013. Phone 1-800-SPRINGER, fax (201) 348-4505, e-mail orders-ny@springer-sbm.com, or visit www.springeronline.com.

For information on translations, please e-mail rights@apress.com, or visit www.apress.com.

Apress and friends of ED books may be purchased in bulk for academic, corporate, or promotional use. eBook versions and licenses are also available for most titles. For more information, reference our Special Bulk Sales–eBook Licensing web page at www.apress.com/bulk-sales.

The source code for this book is available to readers at www.apress.com. You will need to answer questions pertaining to this book in order to successfully download the code.

This book is dedicated to my mother, Edythe Levine, who will not understand one word of it, but will love it anyway.

—Jesse Liberty

This book is dedicated to my wife, Ulrike Stoll, who has been and continues to be infinitely understanding about my late nights spent hacking on the next big idea.

—Paul Betts

Contents at a Glance

Contents

v

About the Authors

 **Jesse Liberty** is a senior developer-community evangelist on the Microsoft Windows Phone team. He hosts the popular "Yet Another Podcast" on his blog at `http://JesseLiberty.com`. The entire blog is required reading. Liberty is the co-author of numerous top-selling books, including *Migrating to Windows Phone 7* by (Apress, 2011) and *Programming C# 4.0* (O'Reilly Media, 2010). Prior to Microsoft, he was a distinguished software engineer at AT&T, a software architect for PBS, and vice president of information technology at Citibank. He can be followed on Twitter `@JesseLiberty`.

 **Paul Betts** is a software developer and Hubbernaut at GitHub, where he works on bringing the joy of Git and GitHub to the world of .NET and Windows. Paul previously worked at Microsoft in the Windows and Office organizations. His blog can be found at `http://blog.paulbetts.org`. Follow him on Twitter at `@xpaulbettsx`.

About the Technical Reviewer

Stefan Turalski is a nice chap who is capable of performing both magical and trivial things with a little help from code, libraries, tools, APIs, servers, and the like. He is experienced in almost all aspects of the software lifecycle, and is especially skilled in business analysis, design, implementation, testing, and QA.

Turalski's areas of interest are wide, best summarized as emerging technologies. His current focus is on .NET 4.5 , GPGPU, event-driven architectures, and software engineering at large. Before he realized that he enjoys criticizing other people's work more, Stefan published several technical articles, mainly about .NET technology, SOA (service-oriented architecture), and software engineering.

For the last ten or so years, Turalski has built solutions ranging from Perl scripts, embedded systems, and web sites, to highly scalable C++/Java/.NET enterprise class systems. Feel free to contact him at `stefan.turalski@ gmail.com`.

Acknowledgments

Thank you to Paul Betts whose genius was the sine qua non of this entire project. Special thanks to John Osborn, Jessica Belanger, Stefan Turalski, Ewan Buckingham, Kimberly Burton and all the folks at Apress for bringing this book to life and making it a far better book than the one we originally wrote. And thank you, dear reader, without whom this book would be a paperweight.

—Jesse Liberty

Thanks to Erik Meijer, Bart de Smet, Wes Dyer, Matthew Podwysocki, and the rest of the Rx team. They have brought their brilliant ideas to life by creating the Reactive Extensions. Thanks to my co-author, Jesse Liberty, for explaining my far too terse samples in a language that human beings can actually understand. Thanks also to our technical editor and the great people at Apress for their hard work in making this a great book.

—Paul Betts

Foreword

For the past fifteen years, like a cyber-age captain Ahab, I have been hunting the unruly, fail whale of web programming. When you move from a single machine to the distributed world of the web, all of your existing assumptions about programming fail to hold. In particular, you suddenly have to face problems such as latency, network errors, and heterogeneity in data models, size, and velocity. You can try to ignore them, but they will invariably come back to bite off your leg.

Whenever I face a seemingly impossible problem like this, I turn to my secret weapon, mathematics, and in particular, category theory. Mathematicians often refer to category theory as "generalized abstract nonsense," which actually is a rather accurate moniker. Category theory is the mathematician's version of interface-based programming. As a result, the true essence of the problem surfaces, un-muddled by implementation details, and as a result, often uncovers unexpected connections between seemingly different concrete solutions. In this particular case, the idea of monads, already discovered and heavily used by the functional programming community to deal with side effects, turned out to be the perfect match to virtualize the variety, volume, and velocity dimensions of programming against collections.

Initially, LINQ—the incarnation of monads in .NET—targeted enumerable, or pull-based, in-memory (LINQ to Objects, LINQ to XML) and remote collections (LINQ to SQL, Entity Framework) with elements of various shapes (object, documents, rows). In the case of pull-based collections, the consumer synchronously requests subsequent items from a local or remote collection, and is blocked while the producer is busy generating the next value. Using the query comprehension syntax in C#, VB, and F#, developers can write declarative and compositional "queries" against enumerable collections, which can either be in-memory, such as an array or a list, or remote, such as a relational database.

Now you may ask yourself what this all has to do with orchestrating and coordinating event-based and asynchronous programs. That is where another mathematical trick comes in. By dualizing the IEnumerable/IEnumerator interfaces for synchronous collections, we get two interfaces, IObservable and IObserver, which characterize push-based, or observable streams. In this case, producers asynchronously notify consumers whenever a new item becomes available in the collection, and the consumer is unblocked to do whatever other work it needs to do between notifications.

The beauty of this trick is that we can use LINQ query comprehensions on either kind of collection. We can filter, transform, group, and join both synchronous, pull-based enumerable collections, as well as asynchronous, push-based observable collections, using exactly the same mechanism. In fact, we can even convert between the two, removing concurrency in one direction, and adding concurrency in the other. That brings us to the idea of schedulers, but you should read about those in the book.

In this book, Jesse and Paul do an amazing job explaining LINQ and the LINQ background of Rx, its relationship to standard design patterns, such as Subject/Observer, and peeking into the fundamental concepts of Rx, such as the IObservable/IObserver interfaces and schedulers. This book provides a wealth of information about applying Rx to real-world problems, such as wrapping .NET events and APM, testing asynchronous programs, using Rx.js in combination with various standard JavaScript libraries, and of course, simplifying the "Model-View-ViewModel Pattern" (note the careful hyphenation).

What I like in particular is that all concepts are clearly illustrated by artfully crafted code examples provided at precisely the right level of abstraction, addressing the topic at hand without leading the reader astray with unnecessary details. Developers can pick up this book and be up and running with Rx in minutes—no scary math required at all. But, you can be assured that everything you learn in this delightful book is built on strong foundations.

— Erik Meijer
Partner-Architect, Microsoft

Introduction

Right now, we as programmers are at an impasse—a transition period between the well-understood world of imperative programming, and a world that is increasingly at odds with this model. In the '80s, everything was simple: one machine, one thread, no network.

CPUs are now scaling horizontally, adding more and more cores, instead of scaling the CPU speeds. Network and disk performance are now increasingly requiring asynchronous I/O in order to build high-performance solutions.

Our tools to write asynchronous code, however, haven't kept up with the rest of the world—threads, locks, and events are the assembly language of asynchronous programming. They are straightforward to understand, but as the complexity of the application becomes larger, it becomes extremely difficult to determine if a given block of code will run correctly with respect to the rest of the application.

We need a way to retain the asynchronous nature of modern applications, while also retaining the deterministic nature of traditional imperative programming.

A compelling solution to these problems is functional reactive programming. This term sounds academic and overwhelming, however, if you've ever written a formula in Excel, good news—you've already done functional reactive programming.

Let's go through that title piece by piece, starting with the word "functional." Many people have a definition of functional programming, often from their college computer science course that covered Scheme or Common Lisp, usually something along the lines of, "it means never using variables."

Instead, think of FP as a *mindset*: "How is the output of my program *related* to my input, and how can I describe that relation in code?" In this book, we'll examine Language Integrated Queries (LINQ), a powerful technology that allows us to describe a result list based on an input list and a set of transformations on that input.

The disadvantage to LINQ is that this technology only works on lists, not data that is incoming or changing. However, there is a type of list that is hiding in plain sight, only disguised—events. Consider the KeyUp event: for every key that the user presses, an object representing the key will be generated— "H"–"e"–"l"–"l"–"o".

What if we thought of an event as a list? What if we could apply everything we know about lists to events, like how to filter them or create new lists based on existing lists?

Reactive Extensions allow you to treat asynchronous sources of information, such as events, and reason about them in the same way that you currently can reason about lists. This means, that once you become proficient with using LINQ to write single-threaded programs, you can apply your knowledge and write similar programs that are completely asynchronous.

A warning: this book is not easy to understand on first grasp. Rx will stretch your brain in ways it's not used to stretching, and you, like the authors, will almost certainly hit a learning curve.

The results, however, are most definitely worth it, as programs that would be incredibly difficult to write correctly otherwise, are trivially easy to write and reason with Reactive Extensions.

CHAPTER 1

Introducing LINQ and Rx

In a sentence, LINQ is a powerful way to interact with and extract data from collections, while Rx is an extension of LINQ targeted at asynchronous collections; that is, collections that will be populated asynchronously, typically from web services or elsewhere in the cloud.

LINQ was introduced to C# programmers with C# 3.0. On the other hand, Reactive Extensions (Rx) is an emerging technology, born in Microsoft DevLabs and adopted as part of a standalone full product from Microsoft in 2011.

We believe that the use of LINQ will expand greatly in the next few years, especially in conjunction with Reactive Extensions. Rx extends many of the principles and features of LINQ to a wide set of platforms (including JavaScript) and will be a vital part of Windows Phone programming, where asynchronous events are the rule. As the data we deal with becomes more complex, LINQ will help bring order and clarity to .NET programming. Similarly, as more and more data is retrieved asynchronously from the cloud, and elsewhere, Rx will help you create simpler, cleaner, and more maintainable code.

In this chapter you will learn why LINQ and Rx are important and you'll examine some of the fundamental operators of both LINQ and Rx. This will provide a context for the coming chapters in which we'll dive deeper into both LINQ and Reactive Extensions.

Note Throughout this book we use Rx as shorthand for Reactive Extensions, just as we use LINQ for Language Integrated Query.

What LINQ Is

LINQ (Language Integrated Query)—pronounced "link"—extends .NET to provide a way to query and transform collections, relational data, and XML documents. It provides a SQL-like syntax within C# for querying data, regardless of where that data originates.

LINQ also brings a much more *declarative* or *functional* approach to programming than previously available in .NET.

■ **Note**   Functional programming is one approach to creating declarative code.

In declarative programming, the logic and requirements are expressed but the execution steps are not.

LINQ and Rx are functional aspects of the C# language, in that they focus more on what you are trying to accomplish than on the steps required to get to that goal. Most programmers find that the functional approach makes it cleaner and easier to maintain code than the more traditional, imperative style of programming.

With the imperative approach, a program consists of a series of steps—often steps within loops—that detail what to do at any given moment. In declarative programming, we're able to express what is required at a higher level of abstraction.

It is the difference between saying on the one hand (imperative): "Open this collection, take each person out, test to see if the person is a manager, if the person is a manager—increase the salary by 20 percent, and put the person back into the collection;" and, on the other hand saying (declarative): "Raise the salary of all the managers by 20 percent."

The imperative style tells you how to accomplish the goal; the declarative style tells you what the goal is. Using concrete programming examples of Rx and LINQ, this book will demonstrate differences that are more declarative than imperative.

What Rx Is

Reactive Extensions provide you with a new way to orchestrate and integrate asynchronous events, such as coordinating multiple streams as they arrive asynchronously from the cloud. With Rx you can "flatten" these streams into a single method, enormously simplifying your code. For example, the classic async pattern in .NET is to initiate each call with a BeginXXX method and end it with an EndXXX method, also known as the Begin/End pattern. If you make more than a few simultaneous asynchronous calls, following the thread of control becomes impossible very quickly. But with Rx, the Begin/End pattern is collapsed into a single method, making the code much cleaner and easier to follow.

Reactive Extensions have been described as a library for *composing asynchronous* and *event-based* programs using *observable collections.*[1]

Let's take a closer look at each of these attributes.

- ***Composing***: One of the primary goals of Reactive Extensions is to make the work of combining asynchronous operations significantly easier. To do this, the data flow must be clarified and the code consolidated so that it is less spread out throughout your application.

- ***Asynchronous***: While not everything you'll do in Rx is asynchronous, the async code you write will be simpler, easier to understand, and thus far easier to maintain.

---

[1] MSDN Data Developer Center, "Reactive Extensions," http://msdn.microsoft.com/en-us/data/gg577609.

- *Event-based*: Rx can simplify even traditional event-based programs, as you'll see later in the book when we examine implementation of drag and drop.

- *Observable collections*: The bread and butter of Rx. An observable collection is a collection whose objects may not be available at the time you first interact with it. We will return to this topic throughout this book. For now, the most useful analogy is that observable collections are to Rx what enumerable collections are to LINQ.

■ **Caution** There is significant potential for confusion between the Silverlight ObservableCollection and Observable Collections in Rx. The former is a specific generic collection and the latter is any collection that implements IObservable, which will be described in detail later in this book.

Getting Rx and LINQ

If you have .NET 4 or later, you have LINQ—it is built into the framework. Similarly, if you have the Windows Phone tools installed, you have Rx for Windows Phone. To obtain the latest edition of Rx for other .NET platforms, you can go to the Rx site (http://msdn.microsoft.com/en-us/data/gg577610) on MSDN. There you will find complete instructions for downloading and installing Rx for Phone, Silverlight, WPF (Windows Presentation Foundation), Xbox, Zune, and JavaScript.

You can also install Rx on a project basis in Visual Studio 2010 (and above) using NuGet. For more information, visit the NuGet project page at http://nuget.codeplex.com/.

Distinguishing Rx and LINQ

LINQ is brilliant at working with static collections, allowing you to use a SQL-like syntax to query and manipulate data from disparate sources. On the other hand, Rx's forté is in working with what we call *future collections*—that is collections that have been defined, but not yet fully populated.

LINQ requires that all the data be available when we first start writing our LINQ statements. That is, to build a new collection with LINQ, we need a starting collection.

What happens, however, if we don't have all the data? Imagine trying to write a service that operates on live, stock-trading data, in which case we want to operate on incoming *streams* of data *in real-time*. LINQ would not know what to do with this, as a stream is not a static collection—its contents will arrive, but they're not there yet, and the timing of their arrival is not predictable. Rx allows us to operate on this kind of data just as easily as we can operate on static data with LINQ.

There is a cognitive boot-strap problem for anyone learning Reactive Extensions, just as there is with LINQ. At first, the Rx code appears confusing and convoluted, and thus difficult to understand and maintain. Once you become comfortable with the syntax and the "mind set," however, the code will seem simpler than "traditional" programming; and many complex problems devolve to rather simple solutions.

The comparison between LINQ and Rx is not coincidental; these are deeply-related technologies. And, you can see the relationship in very practical ways.

In LINQ, we take an input collection, and build a *pipeline* to get a new collection. A pipeline is assembled in stages, and at each stage something is added, removed, or refined—until we end up with a new collection. The truth is, however, that the new collection is really just a modified version of the original collection.

At first glance, collections and streams are very different, but they are related in key ways, which is why we refer to streams as *future collections*. Both streams and collections are sequences of items in a particular order. LINQ and Rx let us transform these sequences into new sequences.

Throughout this book and when you are trying out the examples, always have this question in your head: "How is the sequence that I *want* related to the sequence that I *have*?" In other words, the LINQ or Rx pipeline that you build describes how the output is created from the input.

Why Bother?

After all is said and done, the practical programmer wants to know if the benefits of learning LINQ and Rx are worth the investment of time and effort. What do these technologies bring to the party that you can't get elsewhere?

LINQ and Rx are:

- First-class members of .NET. This allows for full support from IntelliSense and syntax highlighting in Visual Studio and LINQPad.

- Designed to work with all forms of data, from databases to XML to files.

- Highly extensible. It allows you to create your own libraries in order to extend their functionality.

- Composable. As noted, both LINQ and Rx are used to combine and compose more complex operations out of simpler building blocks.

- Declarative. LINQ and Rx bring a bit of functional programming to your code, as described later in this chapter.

- Simplifying. Many constructs that take just a line or two of LINQ or Rx would otherwise take many complex lines of confusing code.

We'll take a closer look at Rx and LINQ throughout the rest of the book, but first, you need to get acquainted with the tools you'll use: Visual Studio and LINQPad.

Choosing your IDE

The examples in this book can be run in any version of Visual Studio 2010 or later, or, with very minor modifications, in LINQPad, a free utility (download at `http://linqpad.net`) that provides an easy way to quickly try out sets of LINQ statements without the overhead of a complete development environment.

Let's look at a simple example, first using Visual Studio and then LINQPad. To begin, open Visual Studio and create a new Console Application named `QueryAgainstListOfIntegers`. The complete source code is as follows:

```csharp
using System;
using System.Collections.Generic;
using System.Linq;

namespace QueryAgainstListOfIntegers
{
    internal class Program
    {
        private static void Main( string[ ] args )
        {
            var list = new List<int>( ) { 1, 2, 3, 5, 7, 11, 13 };
            var enumerable = from num in list
                             where num < 6
                             select num;

            foreach ( var val in enumerable )
                Console.WriteLine( val );
        }
    }
}
```

This small program illustrates a number of important things about LINQ syntax and features that appeared for the first time in C# 3.0 and 4.0. Before we begin our analysis, however, let's take a look at how the tools can make it easy to create and run the code.

You can copy and paste the LINQ statements at the heart of the program from Visual Studio into LINQPad to try them out in that utility. To do this, first set the language in LINQPad to "C# Statements" and copy in the following code:

```csharp
var list = new List<int>( ) { 1, 2, 3, 5, 7, 11, 13 };
var enumerable = from num in list
        where num < 6
        select num;

foreach ( var val in enumerable )
        Console.WriteLine( val );
```

■ **Note**   You do not need the using statements or the method structures; just the LINQ statements that you want to run.

Run this code with Visual Studio and then with LINQPad. You'll see that they both produce the same result, as follows:

1

2

3

5

C# and .NET Fundamentals

Now that you have both tools working, let's take this small program apart line by line and examine the constructs it uses. In the next section, we'll review some features of C# and .NET, whose mastery is fundamental to Rx and LINQ.

Var

Let's consider the program from the beginning. The first line *could* have been written as follows:

```
List<int> list = new List<int>( ) { 1, 2, 3, 5, 7, 11, 13 };
```

The results would have been identical. The advantages of the **var** keyword are that you avoid redundancy and that it is a bit terser. Further, there are times when you, as the programmer, may not *know* the type and letting the compiler infer the type (as is done with **var**) can be a tremendous time-saver—why look up the type when the compiler can figure it out?

Make no mistake, however; variables and objects declared with **var** are *type safe.* If you were to hover your cursor over the variable name list, you'd find that it is of type List<int>, as shown in Figure 1-1.

```
var list = new List<int>( ) { 1, 2, 3, 5, 7, 11, 13 };
     List<int> list ▾
```

Figure 1-1. Showing that list is type safe

You can assign list to another List<int>, but if you try to assign it to anything else (for example, a string) the compiler will complain.

Collection Initialization

A second thing to note in this very first line of the program is the use of initialization for the list.

```
new List<int>( ) { 1, 2, 3, 5, 7, 11, 13 };
```

Initialization follows the new keyword and the parentheses and is surrounded by braces. The initialization has the same effect as if you had it written as follows:

```
var list = new List<int>();
list.Add(1);
list.Add(2);
list.Add(3);
list.Add(5);
list.Add(7);
list.Add(11);
list.Add(13);
```

But again, initialization is easier to read and to maintain.

The following three lines constituted a *LINQ query expression*:

```
var enumerable = from num in list
        where num < 6
        select num;
```

This begins with the use of the keyword **var**, this time for the variable named **enumerable**. Once again enumerable is type safe, in this case the variable **enumerable**'s true type is **IEnumerable<int>**.

The first line of the LINQ query is a *from* statement, in this case creating the temporary variable *number* and indicating that we are selecting from a list of integers named *list*.

The second line is a *where* clause which narrows the answer space to those values that are less than six. The final line is a *select* statement or projection of the results.

The net effect of these three lines of code is that enumerable is an **IEnumerable** of integers that contains all of the values from the list whose value is less than six.

IEnumerable

Because *enumerable* is an **IEnumerable**, you can run a **foreach** loop over it, as done here.

As will be noted many times in this book, **IEnumerable** is the heart of LINQ, and as we will see, **IObservable** is the heart of Reactive Extensions.

IEnumerable is an interface; classes that implement that interface will provide **MoveNext()**, **Current()** and **Reset()**.

Typically you can ignore this implementation detail, as you do when using for each, but understanding how **IEnumerable** works is critical to seeing the connection between Link and Reactive Extensions.

You can, in fact, rewrite the **foreach** loop using the following operators:

```
var e = enumerable.GetEnumerator( );
while ( e.MoveNext( ) )
{
    Console.WriteLine( e.Current );
}
```

This will produce the same result, and in fact, the **foreach** construct should best be thought of as shorthand.

Properties

Properties have the wonderful characteristic of appearing to be member-fields to the client of the class, allowing the client to write, for example, the following:

```
int x = thePerson.Age;  // Age is a property that appears to be a field
```

In this case, Age will appear to the author of the class as a method, allowing the owner of the class to write the following:

```
public int Age
{
   get { return birthdate - DateTime.Now; }
   set { //... }
}
```

Automatic Properties

In a normal property, there is an explicit getter and setter; however, it is very common to find yourself writing something like the following:

```
private int _age;
public int Age
{
   get { return _age; }
   set { _age = value; }
}
```

In this common idiom, you have a backing variable and the property does nothing but return or set the backing variable. To save typing, C# now lets you use automatic properties.

```
public int Age { get; set; }
```

The IL code produced is *identical*—the automatic property is just shorthand for the idiom.

Note that automatic properties require both a setter and a getter (though one can be private) and you cannot do any work in either. That is, if your getter or setter needs to do any work (for example, call a method) then you must revert to using normal syntax for properties.

Object Initialization

Assume that you create a **Person** class that looks like the following:

```
public class Person
 {
     public string FullName { get; set; }
     public string Address { get; set; }
     public string Phone { get; set; }
     public string Email { get; set; }
 }
```

The traditional way to instantiate an object and set its values is as follows:

```
var person = new Person();
person.FullName = "Jesse Liberty";
person.Address = "100 Main Street, Boston, MA";
person.Email = "jliberty@microsoft.com";
person.Phone = "617-555-1212";
```

Object initialization lets you initialize the properties in the Person instance, as follows:

```
var per = new Person()
{
    FullName = "Jesse Liberty",
    Address = "100 Main Street, Boston, MA",
    Email = "jliberty@microsoft.com",
    Phone = "617-555-1212"
};
```

Delegates

Much ink has been spilled attempting to explain delegates, but the concept is really fairly simple. A delegate type is the definition of an object that will "hold" a method. At the time you create a delegate type, you don't necessarily know exactly which method it will hold, but you do need to know the return type and parameters of that method.

A delegate instance is an instance of a delegate type. By creating an instance of the delegate, you can use that instance to invoke the method it "holds." For example, you might know that you are going to invoke one or another method that determines which shape to draw, but you have a number of such methods. Each of these methods returns a string (with the name of the shape) and each takes an integer (used to decide which shape will be drawn). You would declare the delegate type as follows:

```
public delegate string Shaper (int x);
```

You would declare the instance as follows:

```
Shaper s = Shape;
```

Shape is the name of a method. The following is shorthand for:

```
Shaper s = new Shaper(Shape);
```

You would invoke the Shape method through the delegate with the following:

```
s(3);
```

This, again, is shorthand for the following:

```
s.Invoke(3);
```

The result would be identical to calling the following:

```
Shape(3);
```

The following is a complete program you can drop into LINQPad to see this at work:

```
public delegate string Shaper (int x);
void Main()
{
    Shaper s = Shape;
    string result = s( 3 );
    Console.WriteLine( result );

}
 static string Shape(int x)
 {
    if ( x % 2 == 0 )
      return "Circle";
    else
       return "Square";
}
```

Anonymous Methods

Anonymous methods allow you to use an inline, unnamed delegate. Thus, the previous program could be rewritten as follows:

```
public delegate string Shaper (int x);
void Main()
{
Shaper s = delegate(int x)
{
    if ( x % 2 == 0 )
       return  "Circle";
    else
        return "square";
};
string result = s( 3 );
Console.WriteLine( result );

}
```

Lambda Expressions

Anonymous methods are made somewhat obsolete by lambda expressions. The previous could be rewritten as follows:

```
public delegate string Shaper (int x);
void Main()
{
    Shaper s = x =>
    {
       if ( x % 2 == 0 )
          return "Circle";
       else
          return "Square";
```

```
   };
   string result = s( 3 );
   Console.WriteLine( result );

}
```

Lambda expressions are just a shorthand notation for declaring delegates.

To see this at work, let's begin by creating a very simple (if absurd) program that declares a delegate to a method that takes two integers and returns a string, and then uses that delegate to call the method.

```
public MainPage( )
{
   InitializeComponent( );
   Func<int, int, string> AddDelegate = Add;
   string result = AddDelegate( 5, 7 );
   TheListBox.Items.Add( result );
}

private string Add( int a, int b )
{
   return ( a + b ).ToString( );
}
```

Taking this apart, on line 4 we declare `AddDelegate` to be a delegate to a method that takes two integers and returns a string, and we assign that delegate to the `Add` method declared at the bottom of the listing. We then invoke the method through that delegate on line 5, and on line 6 we add the result to the list box we created in `MainPage.xaml`.

Lambda syntax allows us to write the same thing much more tersely.

```
Func<int, int, string> AddLambda =  ( a, b ) => ( ( a + b ).ToString( ) );
result = AddLambda( 3, 8 );
TheListBox.Items.Add( result );
```

The first line (broken over two lines to fit) declares `AddLambda` to be a lambda expression for a method that takes two integers and returns a string, and then replaces the body of the method it points to with what is written to the right of the equal sign. Immediately to the right of the equal sign, in parentheses are the parameters. This is followed by the lambda symbol (`=>`) usually pronounced "goes to" and that is followed by the work of the anonymous method.

Lay them out side by side and the left-hand side is identical, as follows:

```
Func<int, int, string> AddDelegate =
Func<int, int, string> AddLambda =
```

To the right of the equal sign, the method takes its parameters and the lambda takes its parameters, as follows:

```
( int a, int b )
( a, b )
```

The lambda, however, uses type inference to infer the type of the parameters.

The body of the method and the body of the lambda expression are nearly identical.

```
private string Add( int a, int b )
{
   return ( a + b ).ToString( );
}
```

```
=> ( ( a + b ).ToString( ) );
```

Once you have the mapping in your head, it all becomes a trivial exercise, and you quickly become very fond of lambda expressions because they are easier to type, shorter, and easier to maintain.

Note that if you do not have any parameters for the lambda, you indicate that with empty parentheses, as follows:

```
() => ( // some work );
```

Hello LINQ

Let's take a look at another very simple LINQ program in which we extract the even numbers from a list of numbers (which, admittedly, can be done even more easily without LINQ!), as shown in Listing 1-1.

Listing 1-1. Not Hello World

```
List<int> ints = new List<int>()
    { 1,2,3,4,5,6,7,8,9,10,11,12,13,14,15 };
var query = from i in ints
   where i % 2 == 0
   select i;

foreach ( var j in query )
   Console.Write ("{0} ", j);
```

The output is as follows:

```
2 4 6 8 10 12 14
```

The structure of this program is basic to almost any LINQ program. We begin with an enumerable collection (our `List` of integers). The heart of the program is the LINQ query, which begins (always) with a `from` statement and ends (always) with a `select` (projection) statement, as shown here or with `group by`. In the middle are filters (the `where` statement) or one or more of the LINQ operators that we'll be discussing throughout the book.

The result of the query is stored in the local variable query and is itself an `IEnumerable`, which is why you can iterate over it in the `foreach` loop.

We'll say this repeatedly throughout the book: in LINQ and Rx you begin with a collection and you end with a collection.

Hello Rx

The problem with creating your first Rx program is that if it is simple enough to qualify for the job, then it is too simple to do anything more useful than what could be done without it. The following is an example:

```
var input = Observable.Range(1,15);
input.Subscribe(x => Console.WriteLine("The number is {0}", x));
```

As you'll learn in Chapter 3, the Range operator takes two parameters: a starting value and the number of values to generate. In this case, it will generate the numbers 1 through 15. The return of `Observable.Range` is of type `IObservable` of the inferred type `int`. If you hover over the input in the first line —in LINQPad or Visual Studio, but not, unfortunately, in this book—you will see that it is of the following type:

```
System.IObservable<int>
```

As an `IObservable` you can *subscribe* to it, which we do on the second line. The lambda statement can be read as "for each value in the `IObservable` I subscribe to, run the statement `Console.WriteLine(...)`." The output is as follows:

```
The number is 1
The number is 2
The number is 3
The number is 4
The number is 5
The number is 6
The number is 7
The number is 8
The number is 9
The number is 10
The number is 11
The number is 12
The number is 13
The number is 14
The number is 15
```

You'll read much more about observable collections and how to subscribe to them in this and future chapters.

Collections

Both LINQ and Rx work with collections. LINQ works with collections that implement `IEnumerable`, which we will call enumerable collections. Rx works with collections that implement an extension to `IEnumerable`, `IQueryable`, which will refer to as *observable collections*.

The enumerable collection is familiar, as it is the basis for **foreach** loops in C#. Each enumerable collection is able to provide the Next item in the collection until the collection is exhausted. The details of how this is done will be covered later in the book.

Enumerable Collections

Every generic collection provides the ability to enumerate the values. This means that each collection allows you to ask for the first element, then the next, and the following and each element in turn until you stop asking or the collection runs out of elements.

The underlying mechanism is that these collections implement IEnumerable. The IEnumerable interface is as follows:

```
Public interface IEnumerable<T> : IEnumerable
{
    IEnumerator<T> GetEnumerator();
}
```

The GetEnumerator method returns an IEnumerator. The IEnumerator interface is as follows:

```
Public interface IEnumerator
{
    Object Current { get; }
    Bool MoveNext();
    Void Reset();
}
```

You can rewrite Listing 1-1 with an explicit enumerator, as follows:

```
List<int> ints = new List<int>()
    { 1,2,3,4,5,6,7,8,9,10,11,12,13,14,15 };
var query = from i in ints
    where i % 2 == 0
    select i;

IEnumerator<int> e = ints.GetEnumerator();
while (e.MoveNext())
{
    Console.WriteLine(e.Current);
}
```

In fact, the foreach loop is just a shorthand way of writing these examples.

Observable Collections

Rx works with an observable collection, itself based on the Observer design pattern (see the upcoming sidebar).

As noted, a Reactive Extensions observable collection is not the same thing as a Silverlight ObservableCollection control, though both are based on the observer design pattern.

■ **Note** Unless specifically stated otherwise, for the remainder of this book, if we use the term "observable collection," we mean the Rx collection type, not the Silverlight control.

THE OBSERVER DESIGN PATTERN

The Observer design pattern was first codified in *Design Patterns: Elements of Reusable Object-Oriented Software* by Erich Gamma, Richard Helm, Ralph Johnson, and John Vlissides (Addison-Wesley, 1994). The four authors are affectionately known as the "Gang of Four" and the book is often referred to as the "GOF (pronounced *goff*) Book."

The essence of the Observer pattern is that there is an observable object (such as a clock), and there are observers who wish to be informed when the observable changes (e.g., when a second passes).

An `ObservableCollection` in Silverlight implements this pattern in that it automatically raises `PropertyChanged` notifications for any object in the collection that is altered.

The observable collection used by Rx, on the other hand, is a more general implementation of the Observer pattern, allowing for other objects to *subscribe* to any change whatsoever in the collection (including the arrival of new entries).

The term *subscribe* comes from the closely related *Publish and Subscribe* design pattern. In fact, the Observer pattern is a subset of Publish/Subscribe. The observable (clock) can be said to publish certain events (e.g., a clock tick) and the observers can be said to subscribe to those events. This is very much the pattern with event handling in .NET, in which interested objects might subscribe to a button's click event.

For more coverage of the Publish/Subscribe and its patterns, please see the Wikipedia articles at `http://en.wikipedia.org/wiki/Publish/subscribe` and at `http://en.wikipedia.org/wiki/Observer_pattern`, respectively.

Observable Collections vs. Enumerable Collections

Enumerable collections have all their members present at the moment that you are ready to work with them. You can "pull" each item from the collection when you are ready for it, adding, for example, each in turn to a list box.

An observable collection, however, does not have its members available when first created; the members will be added to the collection over time (perhaps by acquiring them from a web service). In this sense, an observable collection is a "future collection." As the members of the observable collection are added, they are pushed out to the subscribers who have registered with the collection, who may then work with these members as they each become available.

In the next section we'll work through an example that will clarify this discussion.

Example: Working with Enumerable and Observable Collections

In this example, we're going to create a pair of `ListBoxes` for a Windows Phone. We'll populate one from an enumerable collection and the other from an observable collection.

The following tells how:

1. Fire up Visual Studio, create a new Windows Phone project, and on the first page divide the Content panel into two columns. Place a `ListBox` in each of the two columns, naming the first list box, `lbEnumerable`, and the second, `lbObservable`.

2. Add a reference to each of the following libraries:

   ```
   Microsoft.Phone.Reactive
   System.Observable
   ```

3. Add a `using` statement, as follows:

   ```
   using Microsoft.Phone.Reactive
   ```

4. Next, we need some data so let's initialize a `List<string>` with the names of the first five American presidents, as follows:

   ```
   public partial class MainPage :
       PhoneApplicationPage
   {
       readonly List<string> names =
           new List<string>
       {
           "George Washington",
           "John Adams",
           "Thomas Jefferson",
           "James Madison",
           "James Monroe",
           "John Quincy Adams"
       };
   ```

■ **Note** Read `List<string>` as "list of string."

This list will be the source for populating both list boxes. We'll do all of the work in a method called `PopulateCollection()`, which we'll call from the page's constructor.

5. In the first part of `PopulateCollection()`, we'll take the traditional approach and iterate through each member of the collection, adding each president's name to the list box. To do that, add the following code in `MainPage.xaml.cs.`:

   ```
   private void PopulateCollection( )
   {
       foreach ( string pName in names )
       {
           lbEnumerable.Items.Add( pName );
       }
   ```

6. To handle the fact that these names might not be immediately available, use the ToObservable() extension method on the list of names, to create an instance of an IObservable collection, as follows:

```
IObservable<string> Observable =
    names.ToObservable( );
```

Note Extension methods are new in C# 4. They allow you to create a static method that appears to extend an existing class, though they are not actually inserted into the class. In this case, the ToObservable appears to extend the generic List class, and can be used just as if it were a method of List<T>.

---

7. ObservableCollection has an overloaded Subscribe method. The first parameter is of type Action<T>, which subscribes a value handler to an Observable sequence. Add the following code to MainPage.xaml.cs, as well:

```
Observable.Subscribe<string>
(
    pName =>
    {
        lbObservable.Items.Add( pName );
    }
);
```

Listing 1-2 illustrates the body of the Action<T>, which in this case is a lambda expression indicating that, given a string, pName, the body of the method adds that name to the appropriate list box. Listing 1-2 is the complete listing.

Listing 1-2. Observable Collection

```
using System;
using System.Collections.Generic;
using Microsoft.Phone.Controls;
using Microsoft.Phone.Reactive;

namespace Observable_Collection
{
    public partial class MainPage :
        PhoneApplicationPage
    {
        readonly List<string> names =
            new List<string>
        {
            "George Washington",
            "John Adams",
            "Thomas Jefferson",
```

```csharp
        "James Madison",
        "James Monroe",
        "John Quincy Adams"
    };

    public MainPage( )
    {
        InitializeComponent( );
        PopulateCollection( );
    }

    private void PopulateCollection( )
    {
        foreach ( string pName in names )
        {
            lbEnumerable.Items.Add( pName );
        }

        IObservable<string> Observable =
            names.ToObservable( );

        Observable.Subscribe<string>
        (
            pName =>
            {
                lbObservable.Items.Add( pName );
            }
        );
    }
}
}
```

Run the program. As you can see, the two lists are identical, even though the second list, handled by Rx, has members that might have been obtained from a web service and thus would not have been available when the program began.

Summary

In this chapter you learned the purpose of LINQ and Rx and saw how Rx extends LINQ. You also saw how IEnumerable is the key interface for LINQ and IObservable is the key interface for Rx. In coming chapters, you'll learn the important operators for both LINQ and Rx, and how to use these technologies to master some of the more important and complex operations in C# programming, such as managing data and handling asynchronicity.

CHAPTER 2

Core LINQ

The relationship between LINQ and Reactive Extensions (Rx) is deep and fascinating. We will explore the relationship between the two in Chapter 5, but for now it is sufficient to point out that the central element in LINQ is `IEnumerable`, much as the central element in Rx is `IObservable`. Many of the same operators appear in both frameworks, such as `Select` and `SelectMany`.

In this chapter we will dive into LINQ in a bit more depth, first exploring the syntax of a LINQ statement, and then a number of useful LINQ operators, and concluding with a demonstration program that will illustrate many of the central concepts of LINQ.

LINQ Syntax

There are a number of flavors of LINQ, each tailored to work with different types of data. LINQ to Objects is designed to work with objects in memory, while LINQ to SQL is designed to work with SQL server-based data. The essence is the same, however, and LINQ to Objects shows that essence particularly well.

Consider the following statements, which you can copy and paste directly into LINQPad:

```
var primes = new List<int>() { 1, 2, 3, 5, 7, 11, 13, 17, 19 };

var query = from num in primes
                    where num < 7
                    select num;

foreach ( var  i in query )
{
   Console.WriteLine(i);
}
```

The central three lines of code compose a LINQ query expression. The body of the query expression begins, as do all query expressions, with the keyword `from`. By placing the `from` clause first, LINQ is able to provide type checking and IntelliSense support.

■ **Note** There is a second syntax used with LINQ, known as *method syntax,* that does not necessarily start with the `from` clause. For example, you might rewrite this query as follows:

```
var query = primes

            .Where (num => num < 7)

            .Select (num => num);
```

The second line in the Query Expression is called the *filter,* and the final line is called the *projection.* The job of the filter is to reduce the answer set, and the job of the projection is to extract the new `IEnumerable` collection from the old.

Let's take a closer look at three additional characteristics of a LINQ statement: its return of `IEnumerable` types, deferred execution, and its powerful collection of operators.

IEnumerable

We are able to iterate over the values in **query** in the previous example (the **foreach** loop) because the LINQ expression returns an `IEnumerable`. In fact, if you hover over the identifier **query** in either Visual Studio or LINQPad you will see that it is identified to be of type `IEnumerable`, as shown in Figure 2-1.

```
foreach ( int i in query )
{   (local variable) System.Collections.Generic.IEnumerable<int> query
        Console.WriteLine(i);
}
```

Figure 2-1. *IntelliSense showing the type of query*

■ **Note** The free version of LINQPad does not offer IntelliSense.

Query Operators

We're going to look at several LINQ operators later in this chapter, but to get us started, examine Listing 2-1, in which we use the **orderby** and **group** by query operators to find all the methods of the **int** type. Note that LINQ automatically uses reflection as needed, to obtain the methods we're searching for.

Listing 2-1. The Code to Copy into LINQPad

```
var query = from method in typeof(int).GetMethods()
        orderby method.Name
        group method by method.Name into groups
        select new
      { MethodName = groups.Key, MethodOverloads = groups.Count() };


foreach ( var item in query)
{
        Console.WriteLine(item);
}
```

The query finds all the methods for int, orders them by name (and the output is alphabetical by method name), and then groups the overloaded methods together (all the methods with the same name), reporting on how many overloads each method has. Figure 2-2 shows the output as rendered by LINQPad.

{ MethodName = CompareTo, MethodOverloads = 2 }	
MethodName	CompareTo
MethodOverloads	2
{ MethodName = Equals, MethodOverloads = 2 }	
MethodName	Equals
MethodOverloads	2
{ MethodName = GetHashCode, MethodOverloads = 1 }	
MethodName	GetHashCode
MethodOverloads	1
{ MethodName = GetType, MethodOverloads = 1 }	
MethodName	GetType
MethodOverloads	1
{ MethodName = GetTypeCode, MethodOverloads = 1 }	
MethodName	GetTypeCode
MethodOverloads	1

{ MethodName = Parse, MethodOverloads = 4 }	
MethodName	Parse
MethodOverloads	4
{ MethodName = ToString, MethodOverloads = 4 }	
MethodName	ToString
MethodOverloads	4
{ MethodName = TryParse, MethodOverloads = 2 }	
MethodName	TryParse
MethodOverloads	2

Figure 2-2. *Output from LINQPad*

Deferred Execution

A key aspect of LINQ is that execution of a query statement is deferred until you actually ask for the first item in the sequence. Consider the following code:

```
var list = new List<int> { 1, 2, 3, 4, 5, 6, 7, 8, 9, 10 };

var query = from num in list
            where num < 7
            select num;

foreach ( var num in query )
{
    Console.WriteLine(num);
}
```

You might at first expect that the code would be evaluated when the LINQ statement is reached. As you can see by running this in a debugger, however, the LINQ statement is not evaluated until the foreach is run. This feature can have both good and bad consequences for the code that you write.

The Good

The following is an example that demonstrates deferred execution by slowing down the requests for evaluation:

```
var q = Enumerable.Range(0, 1000 * 1000)
        .Select(x =>
        {
                Thread.Sleep(1000);
                return x * 10;
        });


foreach (var num in q )
{
        Console.WriteLine(num);
}
```

The query itself evaluates 1,000,000 numbers. For each number, it sleeps one second, and then returns the number multiplied by 10. If we waited for it to evaluate all one million numbers before running the **foreach** loop, we'd have to wait 11.57 days. Fortunately, because of delayed execution, we get a result every second, as you can see by running this code in LINQPad or Visual Studio (note, again, that if you run this in Visual Studio you will need to wrap it in a program structure).

The Bad

Deferred execution can have a downside, as well. In the next example, we set up a LINQ query and then iterate through the results twice. The output may not be quite what we anticipated or want.

```
int counter = 0;
var evenNumbersInSeries = Enumerable.Range(0, 10).Select(x =>
{
        int result = x + counter;
        counter++;
        return result;
});

Console.WriteLine("First Try:\n");
foreach(int i in evenNumbersInSeries)
{
        Console.WriteLine(i);
}

Console.WriteLine("\nSecond Try:\n");
foreach(int i in evenNumbersInSeries)
{
        Console.WriteLine(i);
}
```

The output for these two runs is shown in the following two columns:

0	10
2	12
4	14
6	16
8	18
10	20
12	22
14	24
16	26
18	28

Notice that the second column begins where the first left off. That was not our intention; we expected the two columns to be identical.

We could solve this problem in two ways. One is to reset the counter before running the second loop. Another way to solve this is to *freeze* the evaluation by asking LINQ to convert the results (currently in the variable evenNumberInSeries) to an **array**. The result would be that the entire series would be evaluated and placed in the array and then we'd iterate through the array, as follows:

```
int counter = 0;
var evenNumbersInSeries = Enumerable.Range(0, 10).Select(x =>
{
    int result = x + counter;
    counter++;
    return result;
}).ToArray();

// List the numbers in the series

Console.WriteLine("First Try:\n");
foreach(int i in evenNumbersInSeries) {
    Console.WriteLine(i);
}

// This time, because we added the ToArray(), we'll get the expected result
// every time.

Console.WriteLine("\nSecond Try:\n");
foreach(int i in evenNumbersInSeries) {
    Console.WriteLine(i);
}
```

This code is identical to the earlier version except that we append .ToArray to the LINQ statement. This time when we run the program, both columns are identical. Calling ToArray on the collection causes it to be evaluated and "frozen" in the array, and thus when we iterate over the collection we are iterating over the same array each time.

```
0        0
2        2
4        4
6        6
8        8
10       10
12       12
14       14
16       16
18       18
```

We've been using a number of LINQ operators; let's take a closer look at the most important ones.

Core Operators

A key aspect of becoming comfortable with LINQ is taking advantage of its myriad of available operators. We won't try to provide an exhaustive list, but rather we'll focus on some of the most useful among them.

Any

The operator Any returns a Boolean value and can be used to determine if a sequence is empty or whether it contains a particular predicate.

```
var firstList = Enumerable.Empty<int>();
var secondList = Enumerable.Range(1,10);

Console.WriteLine(
    "The first list has members? {0}, The second list has members? {1}",
        firstList.Any(), secondList.Any() );
```

This code returns the following:

```
The first list has members? False, The second list has members? True
```

Let's add a second test, as follows:

```
Console.WriteLine(
  "Is 6 in the second list? {0}, Is 12 in the second list? {1}",
  secondList.Any(x => x==6),
  secondList.Any(x => x==12) );
```

This second test returns the following:

```
Is 6 in the second list? True, Is 12 in the second list? False
```

■ **Note** Any returns as soon as it finds a match. If we had included 6 in the list three times, Any would return as soon as it encountered the first.

Contains

A second way to determine if a value is in a list is to use the contains operator. This overloaded operator checks to see if a value is in a list. We can rewrite the second test as follows:

```
var firstList = Enumerable.Empty<int>();
var secondList = Enumerable.Range(1,10);

Console.WriteLine("SecondList contains 6? {0}, Second List contains 12? {1}",
secondList.Contains(6), secondList.Contains(12));
```

The results are the same:

```
SecondList contains 6? True, Second List contains 12? False
```

As noted, though the syntax is simpler, the **Contains** operator is overloaded, and you are free to pass in your own comparison method to facilitate comparing items of different types.

To see this at work, create a **Console** Application in Visual Studio. Within the application, create a **Person** class and derived from that, a **Student** class, as follows:

```
class Person
{
    public int ID { get; set; }
    public string FullName { get; set; }
}

class Student : Person
{
    public string Major { get; set; }
}
```

You now create a class derived from **IEqualityComparer**, which will establish whether two **People** are equal or not using whatever you choose as the criteria. You might match **FullName** fields or, more likely, **ID**:

```
class StudentToPersonEquals : IEqualityComparer<Person>
{
    public bool Equals( Person x, Person y )
    {
        if (x.ID == y.ID)
            return true;
        else
            return false;
    }
```

```
    public int GetHashCode( Person obj )
    {
        return obj.GetHashCode();
    }
}
```

With this in place, you can now instantiate a number of **Person** and **Student** objects, and place them in a collection, as follows:

```
static void Main( string[ ] args )
{
    var people = new List<Person>();


    var PaulBetts = new Student()
    { FullName =  "Paul Betts", ID = 1, Major = "Computer Science" };
    people.Add(PaulBetts);

    people.Add( new Person() { ID = 2, FullName = "Jesse Liberty" } );

    people.Add( new Student() {
ID = 3,
FullName = "George Washington",
Major = "Favorite on Fawlty Towers" } );

    people.Add( new Student() {
ID = 4,
FullName = "John Adams",
Major = "History" } );
```

You can now use an instance of your **StudentToPersonEquals** class as the comparer for the **Contains** operator, as follows:

```
Console.WriteLine ("People contains Paul Betts? {0}",
    people.Contains(PaulBetts, new StudentToPersonEquals() ));
```

This allows you to pass in an instance of the **Student** class and have it identified by the **Contains** operator based on the criteria specified in your comparison class.

Take

Take allows you to determine how many objects you'd like to retrieve from what may be a very large collection, as follows:

```
var input = new[] {1,2,3,4,5,6,7,8,9,10,11,12,13,14,15,16,17,18,19,20};
var output = input.Take(5).Select(x => x * 10);

output.Dump();
```

In this case, our source has 20 values. Without the `Take` operator, this code would return the values 10 through 200, but as it is, it returns only the first five of those values, as shown in Figure 2-3.

```
10
20
30
40
50
```

Figure 2-3. The Take operator

Distinct

Often you will have a collection with duplicate values. The `Distinct` operator removes the duplicates and works only on the unique values, as follows:

```
var input = new[] {1,2,3,2,1,2,3,2,1,2,3,2,1};
var output = input.Distinct().Select(x => x * 10);

output.Dump();
```

The following result is the product of just the distinct values:

```
10
20
30
```

Zip

`Zip` is a fascinating operator. It is used to thread two lists together. The easiest way to do it is to call `Zip` on the first list, passing in the name of the second list, and then a lambda statement indicating how you want the lists zipped together. The result of `Zip` is an `Enumerable`.

```
string[] codes = { "AL", "AK", "AZ", "AR", "CA" };
string[] states = {"Alabama", "Alaska", "Arizona", "Arkansas", "California" };

var CodesWithStates = codes.Zip(states, (code, state) => code + ": " + state);

foreach ( var item in CodesWithStates )
{
    Console.WriteLine(item);
}
```

In this case, `CodesWithStates` is an `Enumerable` produced by zipping the two lists, codes and states, together. The output is as follows:

```
AL: Alabama
AK: Alaska
AZ: Arizona
AR: Arkansas
CA: California
```

For the `Zip` operator to work, the two lists do not have to be of the same type, nor of the same length. The following is a quick second example:

```
int[] codes = Enumerable.Range(1,100).ToArray();
string[] states = {"Alabama", "Alaska", "Arizona", "Arkansas", "California" };

var CodesWithStates = codes.Zip(states, (code, state) => code + ": " + state);

foreach ( var item in CodesWithStates )
{
    Console.WriteLine(item);
}
```

In this second case, the codes array is an array of 100 integers. `Zip` puts the two disparate lists together until it runs out of one list (in this case, states), in which case it terminates. The output is as follows:

```
1: Alabama
2: Alaska
3: Arizona
4: Arkansas
5: California
```

SelectMany

One of the most powerful operators in LINQ is also one of the most difficult to understand. The principal use of `SelectMany` is to flatten collections of collections (or hierarchies) into single dimension collections, but as we'll see in a later section, it has other uses as well. Thus, if we have [1,2,3],[4],[5,6] and we run `SelectMany`, the result will be a single collection: [1,2,3,4,5,6].

It is critical to come to a complete understanding of `SelectMany` because the Reactive version is instrumental in helping us chain calls to asynchronous methods. In the following two sections, we'll take a look, first, at its use to flatten hierarchies, and then to recursively traverse them.

Flattening Hierarchies

To better understand the use of the `SelectMany` operator to flatten hierarchies, let's look at two examples.

In our first example, we will create an object, `Book`, which will contain a list of authors.

```
class Book
  {
      public string Title { get; set; }
      public List<Author> Authors { get; set; }
  }
```

```
class Author
{
    public string FullName { get; set; }
}
```

We then create a method to get books and their authors. You might do this by calling into a database or a web service, but we can mock it up using a simple static method that will create the books and return a collection of, in this case, two books, each populated with one or more authors.

```
private static List<Book> GetBooks()
{
    var books = new List<Book>()
    {
        new Book
        {
            Title = "Programming C#",
            Authors = new List<Author>()
            {
                new Author { FullName = "Jesse Liberty" },
                new Author { FullName = "Ian Griffiths" },
                new Author { FullName = "Matthew Adams" }
            }
        },
        new Book
        {
            Title = "Programming Reactive Extensions and LINQ",
            Authors = new List<Author>()
            {
                new Author { FullName = "Jesse Liberty" },
                new Author { FullName = "Paul Betts" }
            }
        }
    };
    return books;
}
```

We're now ready to use LINQ to get the authors of both books, as follows:

```
var books = GetBooks();
var q = from b in books
        select b.Authors;
```

The first line obtains the collection and the next two lines are the LINQ query to obtain the authors of all the books in the collection.

How might we display these names? We could do this with a **for** loop, but q does not contain a collection of authors, it contains a collection of books, each of which contains a collection of authors. To get to the authors, we need nested **foreach** loops, as follows:

```
foreach (var book in q)
{
    foreach (var auth in book)
    {
        Console.WriteLine( auth.FullName );
    }
}
```

The output from these loops is the names of all the authors of both books in the collection, as follows:

```
Jesse Liberty
Ian Griffiths
Matthew Adams
Jesse Liberty
Paul Betts
```

You can accomplish the same thing as the nested `foreach` loops by flattening the hierarchical structure using `SelectMany`.

```
var books = GetBooks();
var q = books.SelectMany( book => book.Authors );
foreach (var author in q)
{
    Console.WriteLine( author.FullName );
}
```

`SelectMany` takes the books collection and flattens it, allowing you to obtain all the `Authors` as if they were in a single, non-hierarchical list.

To replicate this example, create a `Console` application using the complete source code shown in Listing 2-2.

Listing 2-2. Using SelectMany

```
using System;
using System.Collections.Generic;
using System.Linq;
using System.Text;

namespace SelectMany
{
    class Program
    {
        static void Main( string[ ] args )
        {
            var books = GetBooks();

            // alternative 1
            //var q = from b in books
            //           select b.Authors;
            //foreach (var book in q)
            //{
```

```
//      foreach (var auth in book)
//      {
//          Console.WriteLine( auth.FullName );
//      }
//}


// alternative 2
var q = books.SelectMany( book => book.Authors );
foreach (var author in q)
{
    Console.WriteLine( author.FullName );
}
}

private static List<Book> GetBooks()
{
    var books = new List<Book>()
    {
        new Book
        {
            Title = "Programming C#",
            Authors = new List<Author>()
            {
                new Author { FullName = "Jesse Liberty" },
                new Author { FullName = "Ian Griffiths" },
                new Author { FullName = "Matthew Adams" }
            }
        },
        new Book
        {
            Title = "Programming Reactive Extensions and LINQ",
            Authors = new List<Author>()
            {
                new Author { FullName = "Jesse Liberty" },
                new Author { FullName = "Paul Betts" }
            }
        }
    };
    return books;
}
}

class Book
{
    public string Title { get; set; }
    public List<Author> Authors { get; set; }
}
```

```
    class Author
    {
        public string FullName { get; set; }
    }
}
```

■ **Caution** It is imperative that you are comfortable with what SelectMany is doing in this example before you go forward in this book. We strongly recommend taking the complete code and putting it into Visual Studio and playing with it in the debugger. Try replacing SelectMany with Select and see what happens (hint, you'll need a nested foreach loop again).

Our second example will take advantage of SelectMany's flattening to allow for a very clean use of recursion.

Recursively Traversing Hierarchies

The explanation of SelectMany as flattening a hierarchy is correct, and fine as far as it goes, but it is a slight oversimplification. A more complete way to think about SelectMany is, "for each item in this list, I can replace it with nothing, a single item, or another list."

In the example of flattening, we replace each item in each of the three lists with the same item in the output list. But we can also replace each item with two items, or with a function or with just about anything we like.

In the next LINQPad example, we'll use SelectMany and flattening to manage the hierarchy of folders in a directory, allowing us to recurse over each subdirectory in turn.

```
IEnumerable<string> GetFilesInAllSubdirectories(string root)
{
        var di = new System.IO.DirectoryInfo(root);

return di.GetDirectories()
                .SelectMany(x => GetFilesInAllSubdirectories(x.FullName))
                .Concat(di.GetFiles().Select(x => x.FullName));
}

void Main()
{
        var allFilesOnDesktop = GetFilesInAllSubdirectories(
                System.Environment.GetFolderPath(Environment.SpecialFolder.Desktop));

        allFilesOnDesktop.Dump();
}
```

The key line in this program is the second line in the return statement in the GetFilesInAllSubdirectories method, as follows:

.SelectMany(x => GetFilesInAllSubdirectories(x.FullName))

It is critical to understand what this is doing, and how `SelectMany` makes this entire method work.

Let's take this apart line by line. We begin in `Main`, where we call into the recursive method, passing in the folder path to the `Desktop`. We will not return until all the recursive calls are completed.

In the recursive method (`GetFilesInAllSubdirectories`) we begin by getting a `DirectoryInfo` on whatever parameter was passed in (initially `Desktop`). We then call `GetDirectories`, which gives us a collection of all the sub-directories for that directory. `SelectMany` then calls recursively into the same method, passing in the name of each of these subdirectories.

Once we reach the lowest level of subdirectory, we use the Concat operator to add each file name from the call to `GetFiles()`, which we append with `Select` to obtain the full name of the file.

What is critical here is that the `GetDirectories` method returns a hierarchy of directories, and `SelectMany` flattens that into a collection of `Directories` so that we can recurse back into the method with each in turn.

Understanding the LINQ operators is fine and important, but to truly internalize their use, we need a meaningful example.

Example: Parsing a Tab Separated File

A real-world challenge, made more tractable by LINQ, is parsing a delimited file and extracting useful information as if it came from a normalized database. In this next example, we parse the contents of a tab-separated, value text file. The following are the first few lines of the file and its tab-separated fields:

```
name    id      beer_style      first_brewed    alcohol_content original_gravity
        final_gravity   ibu_scale       country brewery_brand   color_srm       from_region
        containers


Miller Genuine Draft    /m/02hv39w


Hakim Stout     /m/059q7h1      Stout           5.8
Harar Beer Factory              Ethiopia
Wellington County Dark Ale      /m/04dqvym                      5.0
        Wellington              Canada  /m/04dr5xv
De Regenboog 't Smisje Honingbier       /m/04dqbhm                      6.0
                Regenboog Brewery               Belgium /m/04dqxph
Hop Back Entire Stout   /m/04dqf8w              4.5
        Hop Back Brewery        United Kingdom  /m/04dqzb7
```

As you can see, the first line has the headings, each separated by a tab. The following lines have the data, though not every line is complete. Incomplete lines have multiple tabs so that, if this page were wide enough, each column would align properly.

Let's see what we can do with this data using a variety of LINQ statements.

We begin by opening the file. Our input data is the raw file as an array of strings, one on each line. We use LINQ to parse the raw data and to calculate statistics.

```
var lines = File.ReadAllLines(@"beer.tsv");
```

First, we want to read the column names from the first line of the file. In a non-LINQ world, we might write code that looks like this, to generate a `Dictionary` whose keys are the column names, and whose values are the index of the column (i.e. "from_region => 6").

```
int i = 0;
var headers = new Dictionary<string, int>();

foreach(var header in lines[0].Split('\t')) {
        headers[header] = i;
        i++;
}

headers.Dump("Imperatively make a dictionary of headers");
```

The output for this non-LINQ version is shown in Figure 2-4.

Key	Value
ne	
id	1
beer_style	2
first_brewe	3
alcohol_content	4
original_gravity	5
final_gravity	6
ibu_scale	7
country	8
brewery_brand	9
olor_srm	10
from_region	11
containers	12
	78

Figure 2-4. Dictionary of headers, imperative

Now let's try that again using LINQ to implement a *functional approach* to a solution. We begin by zipping together the list with the numbers `0..100` (as shown in the following example).

```
headers = Enumerable.Zip(
            lines.First().Split('\t'),
            Enumerable.Range(0,100),
            (header, index) => new {header, index})
        .ToDictionary(k => k.header, v => v.index);
```

```
headers.Dump("The functional version returns the same result");
```

The output is identical, as shown in Figure 2-5. The functional version returns the same result.

Key	Value
name	0
id	1
beer_style	2
first_brewed	3
alcohol_content	4
original_gravity	5
final_gravity	6
ibu_scal	7
country	8
brewery_brand	9
color_srm	10
from_region	11
containers	12
	78

Figure 2-5. Dictionary of headers, functional

Note that this time, instead of calling Zip on one list and passing in the second, we call Zip on Enumerable and pass in both lists. The effect is the same.

> ■ **Note** The key question now is whether the LINQ-based (functional) approach is clearer, simpler, and easier to maintain. Many developers would argue in the affirmative, and they come to use LINQ more and more in their coding. Others feel that LINQ is introducing confusing syntax and making the code *harder* to read. The authors are convinced that LINQ makes for code that is easier to create, read, and maintain, but there is no doubt that there is a learning process as part of the cost.

One of the key features of LINQ (and Rx for that matter) is *composition;* that is, the results of a query can be used by a second query, and a given query can be a clause in a second query.

In short, composability means that input can be transformed into a building block for reuse in further queries. As an example, we'll skip the header and split the lines into fields, with a single line of LINQ code, as follows:

```
IEnumerable<string[]> allRecords =
    lines.Skip(1).Select(line => line.Split('\t'));
```

> ■ **Note** Just as `Take(1)` takes one entry, `Skip(1)` skips one entry, in this case the header.

We can now use this data to parse out reports and other statistics. Starting easy, let's pull out the names of all the countries in the dataset, as follows:

```
var allCountries = allRecords
    .Select(fields => fields[headers["from_region"]])
    .Distinct();

allCountries.Dump("Countries in the dataset");
```

An excerpt of the lengthy list of countries in the output is shown in Figure 2-6.

Countries in the dataset

Ethiopia
Canada
Belgium
United Kingdom
Kenya
Netherlands
United States of America

Figure 2-6. *An excerpt of the countries output by LINQPad*

In the next query we find the five oldest beers. What is particularly rewarding about LINQ (and Rx) is that we can easily see how our results are related to the input records in the dataset; with imperative code, this relationship would be greatly obscured. The code is as follows:

```
var oldestBeers = allRecords
    .Select(x => new { Name = x[headers["name"]], FirstBrewed =
x[headers["first_brewed"]], })
    .Where(x => !String.IsNullOrWhiteSpace(x.FirstBrewed))
    .OrderBy(x => {
        int ret = Int32.MaxValue;
        return (Int32.TryParse(x.FirstBrewed, out ret) ? ret : Int32.MaxValue);
    })
    .Take(5);
```

The output is shown in Figure 2-7.

Name	FirstBrewed
Budweiser Budvar	1265
Franziskaner Hefe-Weisse Hell	1516
Grolsch	1615
Kilkenny	1710
Guinness	1759

Figure 2-7. *The five oldest beers*

Finally, in our most complex query, we calculate which countries brew the strongest beer.

We begin by grouping all the beers by country of origin. Then, for each country, we determine the name of the country and the average beer strength.

We use `Aggregate` to calculate the average. We then use `Where` to ignore records that are missing information to assist with the formatting of the output.

```
var byRegion = allRecords.GroupBy(items => items[headers["from_region"]]);

byRegion
        .Select(group => new {
                Country = group.Key,
                Strength = group
                        .Select(g => g[headers["alcohol_content"]])
                        .Where(x => !String.IsNullOrWhiteSpace(x))
                        .Aggregate(0.0, (acc, x) => acc + Double.Parse(x) / group.Count())
        })
        .Where(x => x.Strength > 0.0)
        .OrderByDescending(x => x.Strength)
        .ThenBy(x => x.Country)
        .Dump();
```

An excerpt of the lengthy output is shown in Figure 2-8.

Country	Strength
Sri Lanka	8
Kosovo	7
Belgium	6.98925619834712
Switzerland	6.9

Figure 2-8. *The countries with the strongest beer*

In this example, you were able to see practical applications of many of the LINQ operators that we discussed earlier in the chapter. As you can see, LINQ can greatly simplify the extraction and manipulation of data from any number of data sources.

Summary

In this chapter, you saw the key role played by `IEnumerable` in LINQ and you worked with a number of the key operators. All of this was brought together in two example programs that used these operators to extricate values and summary information from disparate data sources.

In the next chapter, you'll see that many of the same operators are used in Reactive Extensions, with the difference that rather than creating `IEnumerable` collections, you'll be creating (asynchronous) observable collections.

CHAPTER 3

Core Rx

As noted in previous chapters, Reactive Extensions (Rx) is an extension of LINQ. The key, distinguishing feature of Rx is that rather than being based on `IEnumerable`, Rx is based on `IObservable`—that is, the interface for iterating over an observable collection. This, in turn is based on the Observer design pattern as described in *Design Patterns*.[1]

The essence of the Observer pattern is that the observable object (sometimes called the subject) has actions or properties of interest to one or more observers. When the observable changes in a way that might be of interest to the observers, it notifies them (typically by raising an event).

The nomenclature can be confusing because the Observer pattern is a subset of the Publish and Subscribe pattern, in which a publisher makes information about its state available to one or more subscribers. What truly confounds things is that in Rx, observable collections have *subscribers*—that is, the objects that observe the observable collection are said to subscribe to the collection.

In the case of Rx, an observable collection will notify its subscribers any time an element is added to the collection. This is the essential difference between observable collections and enumerable collections; an observable collection may not have all its members present at the time it is subscribed to; the members arrive and the subscriber is notified.

IObservable and IObserver

As noted in the introduction, the key to Rx is the relationship between an observable collection and the objects that subscribe to that collection. The key interfaces for Rx, comparable to `IEnumerable` and `IEnumerator` are `IObservable` and `IObserver`.

IObservable is defined as follows:

---

[1] Wikipedia, "Design Patterns," `http://en.wikipedia.org/wiki/Design_Patterns`.

```
public interface IObservable<out T>
{
        IDisposable Subscribe (IObserver<T> observer);
}
```

IObserver looks like this:

```
public interface IObserver<in T>
{
        void OnCompleted();
        void OnError(Exception error);
        void OnNext(T value);
}
```

In order to receive notifications from an observable collection, use the Subscribe method and pass in an observer. Note that Subscribe returns an **IDisposable**, which can be used as a handle to stop subscribing to an **Observable**, and Reactive Extensions will handle all of the subscribe and unsubscribe bookkeeping for you.

The **Observer** that you hand to **Subscribe** supports (at least) three methods, as shown in the interface definition. **OnNext** returns the next value in the collection as it becomes available. **OnCompleted** signals the end of the collection, and **OnError** signals that an exception was thrown and offers you an opportunity to handle the error.

Just as LINQ is used to take an enumerable collection and create a new (modified or filtered) enumerable collection, so Rx is used to take an observable collection and create a new observable collection. Many different sources exist for creating observable collections, and you will consider a variety in this and coming chapters.

Example: Creating Observables

Let's start by creating a reusable application to demonstrate a number of different operators.

Start by creating a new Windows Phone Application. Once it is open, add references to **Microsoft.Phone.Reactive** and **System.Observable**.

Add just one control to the XAML file, a **ListBox** with **HorizontalAlignment** and **VerticalAlignment**, both set to **stretch** and with the name **Messages**. You will use this to display the output for each iteration of this program.

```
<Grid x:Name="ContentPanel" Grid.Row="1" Margin="12,0,12,0">
  <ListBox
     Name="Messages"
     HorizontalAlignment="Stretch"
     VerticalAlignment="Stretch"
     Margin="10" />
</Grid>
```

Next, add using statements for **System** and **Microsoft.Phone.Reactive**, as follows:

```
using System;
using Microsoft.Phone.Controls;
using Microsoft.Phone.Reactive;
```

Create a helper method and name it `Observe`. This will be the method that subscribes to the `Observables` that we write and displays the results to the list box. You will invoke this method from within `Main`.

```
private void Observe( )
{
    IObservable<int> source = Observable.Return( 42 );
    IDisposable subscription = source.Subscribe(
        x => Messages.Items.Add( "OnNext: " + x ),
        ex => Messages.Items.Add( "OnError: " + ex.Message ),
        ( ) => Messages.Items.Add( "OnCompleted" )
        );
}
```

The net of this is that whatever values are returned by the `Observable` (including the completion statement and the error statements), will be added to the list box.

Creating an Observable with Return

In our first example, shown in the previous section, you used the `Return` operator, which returns a single value. The result of running this program is that the list box will display the following two lines:

```
OnNext: 42
OnCompleted
```

TESTING IN LINQPAD

LINQPad is a powerful utility for testing and exploring both LINQ and Rx, which we'll be using throughout this book. To run the previous sample in LINQPad, strip it down to its bare essentials; just the following two lines:

```
var input = Observable.Return(42);
input.Dump();
```

This will display the value 42, but will not show the "On Completed" control statement. To see that, add the Reactive Extensions `Materialize()` operator, thus:

```
var input = Observable.Return(42).Materialize();
input.Dump();
```

LINQPad will display both results, the 42 and the OnCompleted, as shown in Figure 3-1.

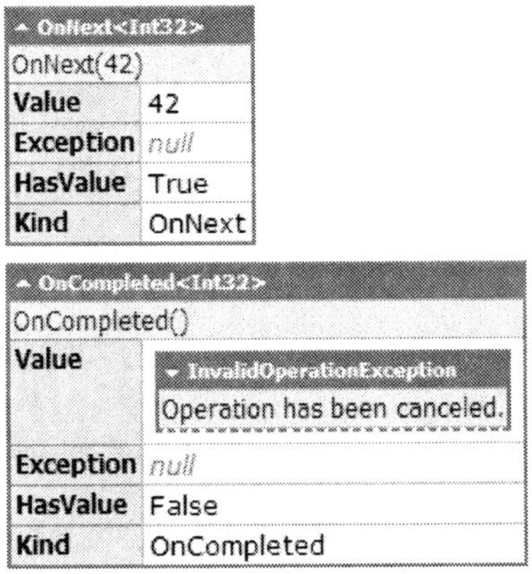

Figure 3-1. *The output of Return and Materialize*

Creating an Observable from Empty

Even simpler than the previous, incredibly simple example is the `Empty` factory method, which doesn't return anything at all. Thus, maintain everything as is, but change the `Observable (Return)` line to say:

```
IObservable<int> source = Observable.Empty<int>();
```

That is, in Visual Studio change the line that says:

```
IObservable<int> source = Observable.Return( 42 );
```

To the following:

```
IObservable<int> source = Observable.Empty<int>();
```

In LINQPad, change the program to read:

```
IObservable<int> source = Observable.Empty<int>();
source.Dump();
```

In Visual Studio the return value this time is just the following single line:

```
OnCompleted
```

In LINQPad there is nothing returned and the program runs to completion with no output.
The practical value of the return and the `Empty` factories will not be apparent until later in this book.

Creating an Observable from a Range

Somewhat more useful than the `Empty` factory is the `Range` factory, which takes two arguments: the starting value and the number of values to generate.

The result is a replaceable statement that reads like the following:

```
IObservable<int> = Observable.Range(42,4)
```

The values in the list box will be

```
OnNext: 42
OnNext: 43
OnNext: 44
OnNext: 45
OnCompleted
```

We might use the Range operator as follows:

```
var input = Observable.Range(1, 100);
input.Sum().Subscribe(x => Console.WriteLine("The Sum is {0}", x));
```

Put these two lines, as is, into LINQPad and set the Language to C# Statements. The output is as follows:

```
The Sum is 5050
```

That is, you subscribed via the Sum operator and used Console.WriteLine as a synonym for LINQPad's dump operator.

Creating an Observable from an Array

We can create an observable from any array with the aptly named ToObservable method. Thus, given an array of integers, you can turn this into an observable collection and then subscribe to that collection, thus:

```
var myArray = new [] { 1, 3, 5, 7, 9 };
var myObservable = myArray.ToObservable();
myObservable.Subscribe(x => Console.WriteLine("Integer: {0}", x));
```

Notice that the compiler is able to infer the type of myArray, even without an explicit "int" in the initialization.

So far we've looked at creating Observables from methods on the Observable class such as Range and Return. Rx also facilitates creating observable collections in other, perhaps less expected ways, as we'll see in the next section.

Creating Observables from Events

One of the fascinating ways you can create an observable collection is from a series of events. In this way the keyboard or mouse can be thought of as a collection of key-presses or mouse movements, respectively.

Example: Searching Wikipedia

A series of events can easily be turned into an observable collection using the `FromEvent` construct. Once more, an example is worth a thousand words, so in our next example, we're going to walk you through an app that makes use of an observable collection of events to capture the user's input and to search Wikipedia with whatever the user has typed. Figure 3-2 shows the output to expect when you run the program.

To get started, open Visual Studio and create a new Windows Phone application named SearchWikipedia. The proximate goal of this application is to search for a term in Wikipedia, but the actual point of this application is to demonstrate creating observable collections from events.

Figure 3-2. *A Windows Phone 7 wiki search app*

Be sure to include the two references and the `using` statement, as described in the previous example. Populate `MainPage.xaml` with the controls shown in Table 3-1 or copy in the XAML code shown in Listing 3-1.

Table 3-1. *XAML Content of MainPage.xaml*

Control	Name	Text	Width
TextBox	Search		Full Width
TextBlock	lblSearch	Searching for...	Full Width
TextBlock	lblProgress	Loading...	Auto
webBrowser	webBrowser1		Full Width

Listing 3-1. *The XAML User Interface Markup for Wikipedia Search Example*

```xml
<Grid
    x:Name="LayoutRoot"
    Background="Transparent">
    <Grid.RowDefinitions>
        <RowDefinition
            Height="Auto" />
        <RowDefinition
            Height="*" />
    </Grid.RowDefinitions>

    <!--TitlePanel contains the name of the application and page title-->
    <StackPanel
        x:Name="TitlePanel"
        Grid.Row="0"
        Margin="12,17,0,28">
        <TextBlock
            x:Name="ApplicationTitle"
            Text="Wikipedia Search"
            Style="{StaticResource PhoneTextNormalStyle}" />
        <TextBlock
            x:Name="PageTitle"
            Text="Find"
            Margin="9,-7,0,0"
            Style="{StaticResource PhoneTextTitle1Style}" />
    </StackPanel>

    <!--ContentPanel - place additional content here-->
    <StackPanel
        Grid.Row="1"
        HorizontalAlignment="Stretch"
        VerticalAlignment="Stretch">
        <TextBox
```

```
      Name="Search"
      Text=""
      HorizontalAlignment="Stretch" />
   <TextBlock
      Name="lblSearch"
      Text="Searching for..." />
   <TextBlock
      Name="lblProgress"
      Text="Loading..."
      Visibility="Collapsed"/>
   <phone:webBrowser
      Name="webBrowser1"
      HorizontalAlignment="Stretch"
      Height="469" />
   </StackPanel>
</Grid>
```

Set the `webBrowser` to be as wide as the page, and to be as tall as possible below the `TextBlocks`.

As already noted, the key to reactive programming is the Observer pattern. This involves an observable and one or more observers. In this case, you want the keyboard entries in the `TextBox` to serve as the observable.

You do not want to react to the text, however, until the user pauses (or stops) typing. You can do all this by converting the `KeyDown` event into an `Observable`, and by using the `Throttle` extension to tell Rx.NET that we're not interested in the text until the user stops typing (defined as half a second passing without a key being pressed).

That latter requirement would normally require setting up a timer, with a call back and a fairly complex bit of code. With Rx, however, you can add a `Throttle` operator, and the timer and related issues are safely hidden away.

Taking this one step at a time, begin by creating an `Observable` from the `KeyUp` event. The syntax is to call `FromEvent` on `Observable`, identifying the type of the arguments and passing in the name of control (in this case `Search`) as well as the specific event you are tracking (`"KeyUp"`). Place the following code in the constructor in `MainPage.xaml.cs`:

```
var keys = Observable.FromEvent<KeyEventArgs>(
   Search, "KeyUp" )
```

You can then apply the `Throttle` operator, as follows:

```
 var keys = Observable.FromEvent<KeyEventArgs>(
   Search, "KeyUp" )
   .Throttle( TimeSpan.FromSeconds( .5 ) );
```

Notice that the `Throttle` operator is added in what is known as the *fluent style*, that is, it is tacked on to the result of calling `FromEvent`. Hovering the mouse over `Throttle` shows that it is an extension method of `IObservable<IEvent<KeyEventArgs>>>`, which is the exact return type of `FromEvent`. You need not worry about that rather frightening type; it is sufficient to know that the type returned by `FromEvent` is the type expected by `Throttle`.

With the `FromEvent` statement in place, you'll create an observable collection named *keys* based on the keyboard entries in the `Search` `TextBox`, after the user stops typing for half a second.

The subscription may observe on a thread other than the UI thread, and if it does so, when you attempt to write to the UI thread, you'll throw an exception due to a Silverlight constraint known as *thread affinity*. It is therefore important that you observe on the UI thread, and to do that, you call `ObserveOn(Deployment.Current.Dispatcher)`, which does the work of ensuring you are on the UI thread.

```
keys.ObserveOn( Deployment.Current.Dispatcher )
```

Now that you are on the right thread, you can call Subscribe.

```
keys.ObserveOn( Deployment.Current.Dispatcher ).Subscribe
```

Each time the user stops typing for half a second, the content of keys will be passed to the body of the Subscribe lambda expression, where you will update the two text fields: (lblSearch and lblProgress) and the web browser.

```
keys.ObserveOn( Deployment.Current.Dispatcher ).Subscribe( evt =>
{
    lblSearch.Text = "Searching for ..." + Search.Text;
    lblProgress.Visibility = System.Windows.Visibility.Visible;
    webBrowser1.Navigate( new Uri( "http://en.wikipedia.org/wiki/"
        + Search.Text ) );
} );
```

Once the browser navigates to the appropriate URI, you want to hide the TextBlock lblProgress and so you'll subscribe to the Navigated event of the browser, which is raised when navigation is complete. When the event is raised, you'll set the visibility to Collapsed.

```
var browser =
    Observable.FromEvent<System.Windows.Navigation.NavigationEventArgs>(
    webBrowser1, "Navigated" );
browser.ObserveOn( Deployment.Current.Dispatcher ).Subscribe( evt =>
    lblProgress.Visibility = System.Windows.Visibility.Collapsed );
```

This little block of code summarizes the "observable from events pattern" very nicely. Let's take it apart to make absolutely certain that you are 100 percent comfortable with every word and punctuation mark in these two lines of code.

- var browser: A local variable to hold the result of FromEvent

- Observable.FromEvent: Obtain an Observable from an event

- <System.Windows.Navigation.NavigationEventArgs>: The type of event you'll be creating the Observable from

- webBrowser1, "Navigated");: The source of the event and the name of the event we're observing

- browser.ObserveOn(Deployment.Current.Dispatcher): Make sure we're observing on the UI thread

- Subscribe: The reason we're here

- (evt =>: The start of the lambda expression, an event is passed in

- lblProgress.Visibility = System.Windows.Visibility.Collapsed);: The work to do; setting the Visibility property to Collapsed

In this example you created an Observable from the KeyUp event and subscribed to the observable collection. Each time text was ready, you had to reach into the TextBox to retrieve the changed text. In the next section you'll refactor the code to simplify this operation by using a LINQ selection statement.

Observable Sequences

Because Observable sequences are first-class objects, you can provide operators over them using generic extension methods. Thus you can modify the code to use a much more LINQ-like select statement to obtain the text as it changes, as follows:

```
var keys = ( from evt in Observable.FromEvent<
                    KeyEventArgs>(
                Search, "KeyUp" )
                select ( ( TextBox ) evt.Sender ).Text )
            .Throttle( TimeSpan.FromSeconds( .5 ) );
```

In this case you are using a query expression to project away the `IEvent<KeyEventArgs>` data type, in favor of a string. As a result, the input sequences are now `Observable` sequences.

You can now rewrite your observe statement, as follows:

```
keys.ObserveOnDispatcher( ).Subscribe( evt =>
{
    lblSearch.Text =
        "Searching for... " + evt;
    lblProgress.Visibility =
        System.Windows.Visibility.Visible;
    webBrowser1.Navigate( new Uri(
        "http://en.wikipedia.org/wiki/" + evt ) );
} );
```

The refactored code is easier to understand and, thus, to maintain. Having taken a look at a solid example of Rx, let's explore some of the Rx operators that you'll be using in your Rx programs.

Rx Operators

Many of the core LINQ operators that were introduced in Chapter 2 have their equivalent in Rx. Let's examine a few of the most common: `take`, `skip`, `distinct`, `using`, and `zip`.

Take

The `Take` operator allows you to specify how many objects you want from the collection. A small example makes this clear,

```
var input = new[] {1,2,3,4,5,4,3,2,1}.ToObservable();
var output = input.Take(5).Select(x => x * 10);

output.Dump();
```

The `Take` operator limits the output of this Rx query to just the first five values. The following is the output:

10

20

30

40

50

Skip

We won't be surprised to learn that Skip allows you to skip over the first n items in the new collection. This can be particularly helpful when you want to skip over, for example, the first row in a collection that contains header information. The following is a simple example to demonstrate the syntax:

```
var input = new[] {1,2,3,4,5,4,3,2,1}.ToObservable();
var output = input.Skip(6).Select(x => x * 10);

output.Dump();
```

This produces the following output:

30

20

10

Distinct

As is true in LINQ Distinct in Rx picks out the distinct values from your collection, as shown:

```
var input = new[] {1,2,3,4,5,4,3,2,1}.ToObservable();
var output = input.Distinct().Select(x => x * 10);
output.Dump();
```

Distinct, in this case, cuts the collection down to the distinct values (1,2,3,4,5) and then selects with the multiplication. Thus the output is as follows:

10

20

30

40

50

Using

While Rx will clean up after itself, it is still your responsibility to manage limited resources, and to dispose of any unmanaged resources.

You can, however, use a variant on the using statement with Observables. To do so, call the static parameterized Using method on Observable. This returns an IObservable<char> and takes two parameters. The first parameter is a Func that returns a streamReader and the second is a Func that takes the StreamReader produced by the first and returns an IObservable of char.

The template parameters are the type of Observable to be produced (in this case char) and the resource to be disposed of when the observable sequence is disposed of (in this case a stream).

```
var ObservableStrings = Observable.Using<char, StreamReader>
(
)
```

The first of the two parameters will create the streamReader and open a FileStream on a text file in the same directory as the program, as follows:

```
() => new StreamReader(new FileStream("randomstrings.txt", FileMode.Open)),
```

The second parameter uses the streamReader just created and reads through the stream to the end (creating a string array). That array is then turned into an observable by calling ToObservable on it, as follows:

```
streamReader =>
(
        from str in streamReader.ReadToEnd()
        select str
)
.ToObservable()
```

You can then subscribe to the newly created ObservableStrings and display the strings found in the text document. The following is the complete program ready to drop into LINQPad.

```
void Main()
{
    var ObservableStrings = Observable.Using<char, StreamReader>
    (
        () => new StreamReader(new FileStream("randomstrings.txt", FileMode.Open)),
        streamReader =>
        (
```

```
            from str in streamReader.ReadToEnd()
            select str
        )
        .ToObservable()
    );

    ObservableStrings.Subscribe(Console.Write);

}
```

Zip

Zip is very similar to Zip in LINQ (see Chapter 2). Once again it is used to thread two collections together; this time, two observables. The following shows an example:

```
var listOne = Observable.Range(1,100);
string[] states = {"Alabama", "Alaska", "Arizona", "Arkansas", "California" };
var listTwo = states.ToObservable();

var numberedStates = listOne.Zip(listTwo,
        (num, state) => num + ": " + state);

numberedStates.Dump();
```

listOne and listTwo are both observables. We create a new collection (numberedStates) by calling the Zip method on listOne. You can see from Figure 3-3 that Zip expects two parameters (the second IObservable (states) and a function that takes an integer and an instance of the type of the second observable) and returns a result. You opt to pass in a lambda expression that resolves to this function signature, passing in an integer and a string (the type used in the second collection).

```
listOne.Zip(
```

```
▲ 1 of 2 ▼ (extension) IObservable<TResult> Observable.Zip (this IObservable<int> first,
                IObservable<TSecond> second,
                Func<int,TSecond,TResult> resultSelector)
    second: Second observable source.  F1 for help
```

Figure 3-3. *The Zip method signature and return type*

Notice that one characteristic of Zip is that it only matches as long as there is a corresponding value in both lists. Even though listOne has 100 values, only the first five are used, as that is the length of listTwo. The following shows the output:

```
1: Alabama
2: Alaska
3: Arizona
4: Arkansas
5: California
```

With these operators under your belt, let's take a look at a more complex Rx example, one in which we convert events to an observable collection.

Example: Drag and Drop

This section is based on a video, *Writing Your First Rx Application*, posted by the Rx Team,[2] one we very much like because it treats your mouse as an observable collection of locations. You can then subscribe to that collection and as new locations (points) become available, you will be notified.

To get started, let's create a new Windows Phone application. Replace the grid with a canvas, and add a `TextBlock` and an image, as shown in the following code:

```
<Canvas>
    <TextBlock
        Name="textBlock"
        Text="Rx for Silverlight" />
    <Image
        Name="image"
        Source="avatar.png"
        Width="191"
        Height="206"
        Canvas.Left="12"
        Canvas.Top="50" />
</Canvas>
```

Note that you will need to download `avatar.png` from the source code listed on www.apress.com or you will want to replace it with an image of your own (a jpeg will work just as well).

The goal is to create observable collections of `MouseDown`, `MouseUp` and especially `MouseMove` events. For each of these three you'll use the `Observable.FromEvent` construct. Place these in the constructor, as follows:

---

[2] Microsoft Channel 9, "Writing your first Rx Application,"
`http://channel9.msdn.com/Blogs/J.Van.Gogh/Writing-your-first-Rx-Application.`

```
var mousedown = from evt in Observable.FromEvent
                    <MouseButtonEventArgs>(
                    image, "MouseLeftButtonDown" )
                select evt.EventArgs.GetPosition( image );

var mouseup = Observable.FromEvent
            <MouseButtonEventArgs>(
            this, "MouseLeftButtonUp" );

var mousemove = from evt in Observable.FromEvent
                    <MouseEventArgs>(
                    this, "MouseMove" )
                select evt.EventArgs.GetPosition(
                    this );
```

Notice that the MouseDown event takes as its parameter the image, rather than the class. You only care when the user clicks on the image itself. MouseUp and MouseMove, on the other hand, do not use the image because you don't want to restrict movement to the image, but rather to the entire canvas.

The fun happens in the query that you can create once you have these collections. Our goal is to create a new (unnamed) class to hold the deltas for each movement until you receive a MouseUp.

```
var q = from start in mousedown
        from end in mousemove.TakeUntil( mouseup )
        select new
        {
            X = end.X - start.X,
            Y = end.Y - start.Y
        };
```

Hovering the mouse over q reveals it to be an IObservable<anonymous>, and thus you can subscribe to it, using the values you retrieve from the unnamed (anonymous) classes you created, as follows:

```
q.Subscribe( value =>
{
    Canvas.SetLeft( image, value.X );
    Canvas.SetTop( image, value.Y );
} );
```

The following is the complete code listing for context:

```
using System.Windows.Controls;
using System.Windows.Input;
using Microsoft.Phone.Controls;
using Microsoft.Phone.Reactive;

namespace MouseTrapDragAndDrop
{
    public partial class MainPage : PhoneApplicationPage
    {
```

```
public MainPage( )
{
    InitializeComponent( );
    var mousedown = from evt in Observable.FromEvent
                            <MouseButtonEventArgs>(
                            image, "MouseLeftButtonDown" )
                        select evt.EventArgs.GetPosition( image );

    var mouseup = Observable.FromEvent
                    <MouseButtonEventArgs>(
                    this, "MouseLeftButtonUp" );

    var mousemove = from evt in Observable.FromEvent
                            <MouseEventArgs>(
                            this, "MouseMove" )
                        select evt.EventArgs.GetPosition(
                            this );

    var q = from start in mousedown
            from end in mousemove.TakeUntil( mouseup )
            select new
            {
                X = end.X - start.X,
                Y = end.Y - start.Y
            };

    q.Subscribe( value =>
    {
        Canvas.SetLeft( image, value.X );
        Canvas.SetTop( image, value.Y );
    } );
    }
  }
}
```

Summary

In this chapter, you learned a number of the key Rx operators and you saw Rx applied to solve the specific problem of drag and drop. In coming chapters, you'll learn more advanced operators and see how Rx can be applied not only to events, but to overt, asynchronous operations.

CHAPTER 4

Practical Rx

The lifeblood of Rx is managing asynchronous tasks without the indirection and potential confusion of non-Rx C# programs. Without Rx, it is common to have asynchronous callbacks that make asynchronous calls to other asynchronous callbacks, creating spaghetti code; the very reason we don't use GoTo very much anymore. With Rx your asynchronous code can be packed into a single method, making for more readable and maintainable code.

In Chapter 3, you saw some of the core operators of Rx; here in Chapter 4, you'll learn how to apply these core concepts of creating working applications. We'll take a look at some of the more advanced operators and then we'll dig deep into a more extensive example.

We begin with a discussion of asynchronous techniques and end with a full demonstration of a working asynchronous Rx program, in which we will build and dissect an application to retrieve images from Bing, based on a select set of keywords using Reactive Extensions.

Let's get started.

Implementing Asynchronous Calls

Let's start by examining a simple synchronous program that will serve as a jumping-off point for some of the more advanced operators. Listing 4-1 shows a very simple synchronous method. Like all the examples in this chapter, Listing 4-1 should be run in LINQPad.

Listing 4-1. A Synchronous Method

```
void Main()
{
  int x = 4;
  int y = 5;
  int z = AddTwoNumbers(4,5);
  z.Dump();
}

int AddTwoNumbers(int a, int b)
{
  return a + b;
}
```

The call to AddTwoNumbers is synchronous, meaning that the processing of Main will pause while AddTwoNumbers is run, not processing the next line (in which the result is output) until the call returns.

Using Observable.Start

Synchronous methods block; and most often this is either undesirable or unacceptable. You can fix this by making the method asynchronous. One of the easiest ways to do this is to call it through IObservable.Start, allowing Rx to manage the asynchronicity, as shown in Listing 4-2.

Listing 4-2. Making a Method Asynchronous Using Observable.Start

```
void Main()
{
        AddTwoNumbersAsync (5,4)
        .Subscribe(x=>Console.WriteLine(x));

}
IObservable<int> AddTwoNumbersAsync(int a, int b)
{
        return Observable.Start(() => AddTwoNumbers(a, b));
}
int AddTwoNumbers(int a, int b)
{
   return a + b;
}
```

Using Observable.Return

Alternatively, you can make any method fit the async signature by using Observable.Return, as shown in Listing 4-3.

Listing 4-3. Making Your Program Appear Asynchronous Using Observable.Return

```
void Main()
{
        AddTwoNumbersObservable (5,4)
        .Subscribe(x=>Console.WriteLine(x));

}
IObservable<int> AddTwoNumbersObservable(int a, int b)
{
        // This runs in the current thread,
        // *not* in the background
        return Observable.Return(AddTwoNumbers(a, b));
}
int AddTwoNumbers(int a, int b)
{
   return a + b;
}
```

Using SelectMany

You can use these async methods along with `SelectMany` to pipe the results of one async method into another, as shown in Listing 4-4.

Listing 4-4. Using SelectMany to Pipe the Results of One Async Method into Another

```
void Main()
{
   AddTwoNumbersAsync(5, 10)
       .SelectMany(aPlusB => MultiplyByFiveObservable(aPlusB))
       .Subscribe(x => Console.WriteLine(x));
}

IObservable<int> AddTwoNumbersAsync(int a, int b)
{
       return Observable.Start(() => AddTwoNumbers(a, b));
}
IObservable<int> MultiplyByFiveObservable(int x)
{
       return Observable.Return(MultiplyByFive(x));
}

int MultiplyByFive(int x)
{
   return x * 5;
}

int AddTwoNumbers(int a, int b)
{
  return a + b;
}
```

Using FromAsyncPattern

The `FromAsyncPattern` operator allows you to create a single Rx method that does the work that would otherwise be done using asynchronous callback methods (the Begin/End pattern in .NET programming).

Let's take a complicated use of the `FromAsyncPattern` and wrap it in a nicer version of an async method. For example, let's assume we have a synchronous version of the Microsoft Translator developer offerings at `www.microsofttranslator.com/dev/`. The synchronous method looks like the following:

```
public string Translate(TranslateRequest request);
The matching asynchronous methods are,
public IAsyncResult BeginTranslate(
    TranslateRequest request, AsyncCallback callback, object context);
public string EndTranslate(IAsyncResult asyncResult);
```

Let's assume that we only want to translate from English to Spanish. We can encapsulate the two asynchronous methods into a simpler method. We'll want a signature that looks as follows:

```
IObservable<string> TranslateToSpanishAsync(
  this LanguageServiceClient client, string englishText);
```

To do this, we want to call the `BeginTranslate` and `EndTranslate` methods, but fill in some defaults. More important, we're going to use an `asyncSubject` instance that we'll name `subject`.

The value of `subject` is seen by considering what would happen if you were to subscribe to the `Observable`, but you did so after the result came back. You'd miss the result because it is a *hot* observable. `asyncSubject` replays the last result, solving this race condition. It effectively creates a *cold* observable, as shown in Listing 4-5.

Listing 4-5. *Using BeginTranslate and EndTranslate*

```
IObservable<string> TranslateToSpanishAsync(
    this LanguageServiceClient client, string englishText)
{
    var subject = new AsyncSubject<string>();

    const string appId = "YourAppIdHere";
    client.BeginTranslate(
     new TranslateRequest(appId, englishText, "en", "es"), asyncResult =>
     {
        try
        {
            string translatedText = client.EndTranslate(asyncResult);
            subject.OnNext(translatedText);
            subject.OnCompleted();
        }
        catch (Exception ex) {
            subject.OnError(ex);
        }
    }, null);

    // This actually returns immediately, before the translate finishes!
    return subject;
}
```

The process of turning Begin/End methods into IObservable-based methods is so mechanical and so frequently needed that Rx has a method that will do it for you automatically.

The FromAsyncPattern method is a little tricky at first glance. FromAsyncPattern returns a Func, specifically it returns an IObservable<TResult>.

We determine the template parameters by looking at the synchronous version of the method. A Func<TranslateRequest string matches the Translate() method shown in Listing 4-5 and reproduced as follows:

```
public string Translate(TranslateRequest request);
```

When you call the Func that is returned, Rx handles the Begin/End calls for you and returns an IObservable, just like the method did by hand. This greatly simplifies the task for you, both demonstrating the advantage of Rx and easing the transition to an Rx-based mind-set.

```
IObservable<string> TranslateToSpanishAsync(
    this LanguageServiceClient client, string englishText)
{
    Func<TranslateRequest, IObservable<string>> translateFunc =
        Observable.FromAsyncPattern<TranslateRequest, string>(
            client.BeginTranslate, client.EndTranslate);

    const string appId = "YourAppIdHere";
    return translateFunc(
        new TranslateRequest(appId, englishText, "en", "es"));
}
```

Let's put to work this translation of the Async pattern to a single Rx-based method in a practical example and then dissect that example.

Example: Programming Asynchronous Interactions With Rx

We're going to build a small program called BingImageSearchDemo to demonstrate how FromAsyncPattern can be used in a practical application.

BingImageSearchDemo allows a user to type a phrase into the search box with the results displaying matching images from Bing, as shown in Figure 4-1. The images are retrieved asynchronously and placed into an observable collection.

Figure 4-1. *The sample program BingImageSearchDemo at work*

To create `BingImageSearchDemo`, we'll need to establish a connection to the Bing Search Engine and we'll need to handle the asynchronous operation of searching and retrieving the results—a perfect job for Reactive Extensions.

We'll approach this step-by-step, building the application as we go, with the full source code available at the end of the chapter.

The steps to building this application are:

- Create a new WPF application

- Add a reference to the Reactive Extension DLLs

- Add the Bing service reference

- Get an API key and place it in the program

- Create the UI

- Create the Rx function prototypes

- Implement the Rx-based `SearchBingAPI`

- Add an event handler for the Search button

- Implement `CreateImageFromURL`

If you'd like to examine the source in detail before reading the commentary, please feel free to skip ahead and then return here when you're done. We'll wait. We're not in a rush.

To get started, create a new WPF application (we could have done this in Silverlight, of course, but at the time of this writing, the WPF version of Rx was a bit more stable).

Begin by adding a reference to the Reactive Extension DLLs, wherever you have stored them on your disk, as shown in Figure 4-2.

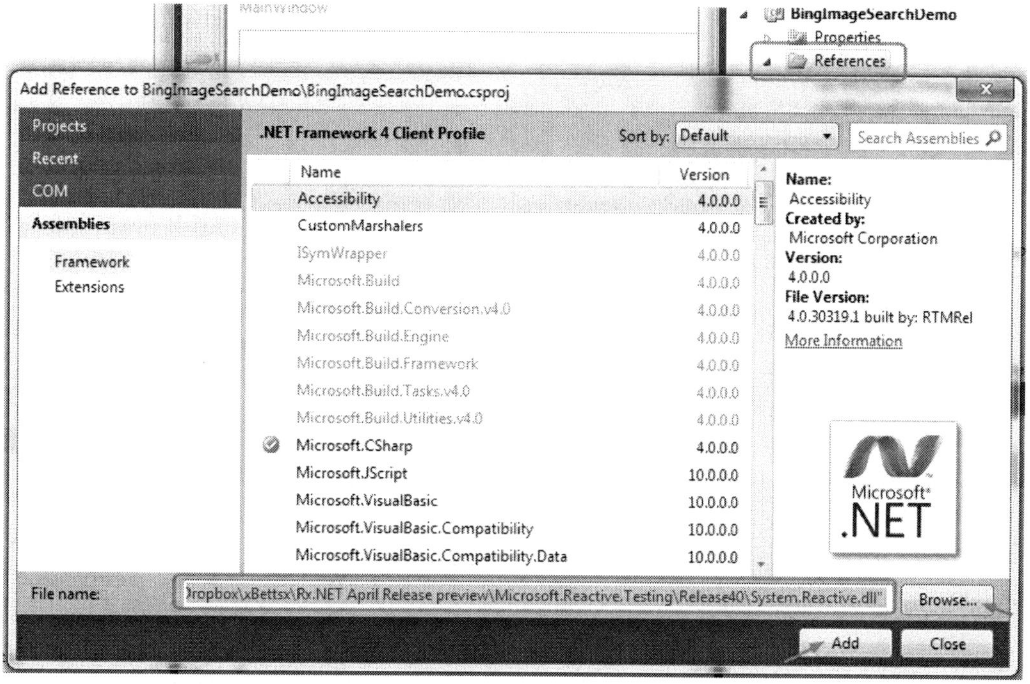

Figure 4-2. Adding references for BingImageSearchDemo

Add the Bing Service Reference

With the Rx reference in place, add a service reference to the Bing API, which you'll find at `http://api.search.live.net/search.wsdl`. Click the Go button and you should see `BingService`. Be sure to click the Advanced button so that you can check the "Generate asynchronous operations" checkbox.

Web services are a classic place to use asynchronous calls, a response from a web service is, by its nature, throttled by the user's web connection. Blocking on a web service call can be fatal (and is prohibited in Windows Phone programming).

We want the asynchronous methods to be generated because we'll use them later (in `Observable.FromAsyncPattern`) to create Rx-friendly methods that will not require callbacks, and that will use fewer resources (since they don't require a thread to wait on a web response). In short, note that we ask for these to be generated, but when the time comes we'll use them only to convert them to Rx methods, not in and of themselves, as shown in Figure 4-3.

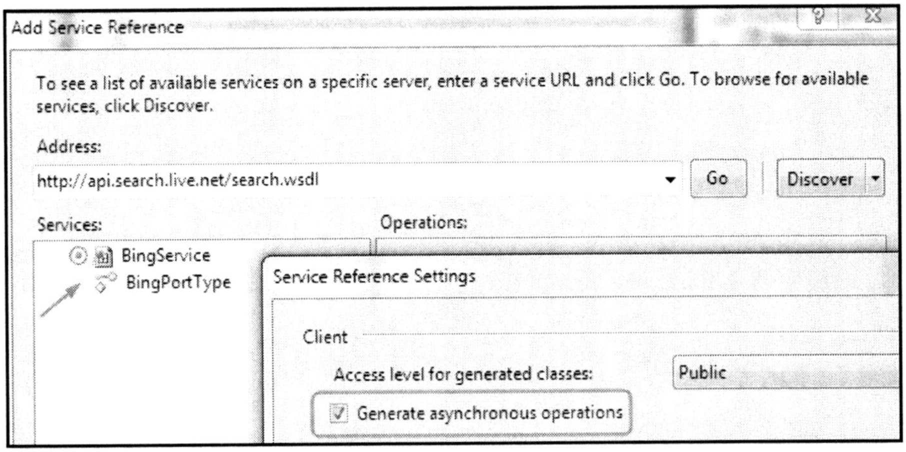

Figure 4-3. *Add a reference to the Bing service*

Before clicking OK, name the service `BingSearch`. You will need a Bing API key, which is easily obtained from the Bing Developer Center at `www.bing.com/developers`.

Place your new key into `App.xaml.cs`,

```
public partial class App : Application
{
    public const string BingSearchKey = "8E...59";
}
```

With the libraries in place, we are ready to create the user interface.

Create the UI

The user interface that we'll build is very simple, as you can see in Figure 4-4. A search box, a button to start the search, and a list box of images to display the results are all that are needed.

Figure 4-4. The user interface for BingImageSearchDemo

To build the user interface, open `MainWindow.xaml` and use the following markup to create our simple interface:

```
<Window x:Class="BingImageSearchDemo.MainWindow"
        xmlns="http://schemas.microsoft.com/winfx/2006/xaml/presentation"
        xmlns:x="http://schemas.microsoft.com/winfx/2006/xaml"
        Title="MainWindow" Height="350" Width="525">

    <Grid
        Margin="16">

        <Grid.RowDefinitions>

            <RowDefinition
                Height="Auto" />

            <RowDefinition
                Height="*" />

        </Grid.RowDefinitions>


        <Grid.ColumnDefinitions>

            <ColumnDefinition
                Width="*" />
```

```
            <ColumnDefinition
                Width="Auto" />

        </Grid.ColumnDefinitions>

        <TextBox
            x:Name="SearchBox" />

        <Button
            x:Name="SearchButton"
            Grid.Column="1"
            Content="Search"
            Margin="8,0,0,0"
            Width="50" />


        <ListBox
            x:Name="Results"
            Grid.Row="1"
            Grid.ColumnSpan="2"
            Margin="0,8,0,0" />

    </Grid>
</Window>
```

With the UI in place, we turn now to implementing the program's functionality, starting by prototyping the two key methods.

Stub the Rx.NET Function Prototypes

We now turn to creating the prototypes for the two key functions we'll be using in this program, one to search for images and the other to display them as they're discovered. Open `MainWindow.xaml.cs` and add the following bit of code:

```
IObservable<string> searchBingImageApi( string query )
{
}

BitmapImage createImageFromUrl( string url )
{
}
```

The method `searchBingImageApi` is used to search for images matching the query. The method `createImageFromURI` is a helper method that creates each image from the URI returned.

We're now ready to implement these prototypes.

Implement the Rx.NET Prototypes

Let's examine to the first of the methods, `searchBingImageAPI`.

```
IObservable<string> searchBingImageApi( string query )
```

The goal of `searchBingImageApi` is to create a future set of contents; that is, contents that are not currently available but will be available in the future on an asynchronous basis. In Rx, we create a future collection by invoking methods that create or return an `IObservable`. An `IObservable` is, quite literally, a collection whose contents will be populated asynchronously.

This is in some ways the crux of the entire demo program and the essence of Rx itself. The `IObservable<string>` that the `searchBingImageAPI` method returns is a collection of future strings, and those strings will be populated by work done in `searchBingImageApi` itself. Let's take a look at that method now.

Implement SearchBingImageApi

The method `searchBingImageApi` begins by instantiating a new `SearchRequest` object.

```
SearchRequest searchRequest = new SearchRequest( );
```

■ **Note** When you first add the upcoming code in this section, you will see many "red squiggly" lines indicating that Visual Studio doesn't know how to resolve some of the identifiers in the code. For all but one of these, you can put the cursor on the troublesome word, hit Ctrl+Period, and Visual Studio will identify and offer to add the necessary `using` statement. Gotta love Visual Studio. The one exception is `getUrlsFromsearchResult`, which is a method that you'll need to stub out for now.

By this point you may be confused as to whether this type was created by Bing, by Rx, or will be created by us. To find out, however, place the cursor over the type, as shown in Figure 4-5.

Figure 4-5. Visual Studio showing the type for SearchRequest

You can immediately see that this is a type defined by Bing. On line 2, we set the `AppId` of the `SearchRequest` object to the `BingSearchKey` we set in `App.xaml.cs`.

```
searchRequest.AppId = App.BingSearchKey;
```

On the next line, we assign the query received as a parameter to the query property of the `SearchRequest`.

```
searchRequest.Query = query;
```

Our next task is to set the *type* of the search; in other words, do we want a text search, an image search, and so forth. As you can see, an image search is indicated by the second offset (offset 1) in the SourceType array.

```
searchRequest.Sources = new SourceType[ 1 ];
searchRequest.Sources[ 0 ] = SourceType.Image;
```

Finally, we instantiate a `BingPortTypeClient`.

```
BingPortTypeClient client = new BingPortTypeClient( );
```

At this point, without Rx we would call into an asynchronous function and get our results in a callback. Instead, we can create an `IObservable` (an observable collection) from the asynchronous methods by using the Reactive Extensions method `FromAsyncPattern`, as follows:

```
Func<SearchRequest, IObservable<SearchResponse>> observableSearchFunc =
    Observable.FromAsyncPattern<SearchRequest, SearchResponse>( client.BeginSearch, client.E
ndSearch );
```

We'll discuss `FromAsyncPattern` in detail in coming chapters, but its essence is that it creates a single function that returns an observable from the async methods:

Our goal, therefore, is to create a method that returns a future collection (an `IObservable`) of `SearchResponse`, as indicated by taking apart the declaration and looking only at the return type, as follows:

```
Func<SearchRequest, IObservable<SearchResponse>>
```

The Reactive Extensions method `FromAsyncPattern` turns Begin/End pairs into a method that returns such a function. Thus we give the `Func` we're creating a name and assign to it the result of invoking `Observable.FromAsyncPattern`, as follows:

```
Func<SearchRequest, IObservable<SearchResponse>> observableSearchFunc =
    Observable.FromAsyncPattern<...>( ... );
```

If we examine the non-asynchronous version of the web service accessors, we'll find that the syntax is to pass in a `SearchRequest` and return an `IObservable<SearchResponse>`. These become the parameterized types, as follows:

```
Func<SearchRequest, IObservable<SearchResponse>> observableSearchFunc =
    Observable.FromAsyncPattern<SearchRequest, SearchResponse>( ...);
```

We then examine the asynchronous version and find the methods that we would call (`client.BeginSearch` and `client.EndSearch`) and they become the arguments to the function, as follows:

```
Func<SearchRequest, IObservable<SearchResponse>> observableSearchFunc =
    Observable.FromAsyncPattern<SearchRequest, SearchResponse>( client.BeginSearch, client.En
dSearch );
```

Examining the entire statement, you can read it aloud as follows: "observableSearchFunc is of type Func that takes one argument of type SearchRequest and returns an IObservable of SearchResponse. Assign to it the results of calling Observable.FromAsyncPattern of SearchRequest and SearchResponse, passing in delegates to client.BeginSearch and client.EndSearch."

Whew!

Since the search will return multiple items for each search request, we'll get back an observable collection of a collection. We can turn that into an observable collection (and thus flatten the results) by using the `SelectMany` operator, (see Chapter 1 for a full explanation of `SelectMany`),

```
return observableSearchFunc( searchRequest )
    .SelectMany( response => getUrlsFromSearchResult( response )
  .ToObservable( ) );
```

You can see that we use SelectMany to take each response and call getUrlsFromSearchResult (to be implemented in the next section), passing in the response, and then taking the result and calling ToObservable() on it, thus matching the signature of being a Func that takes a SearchRequest and returns an IObservable of SearchResponse.

Implement getUrlsFromSearchResults

The implementation of the getUrlsFromSearchResult method is straightforward, as shown in the following:

```
private string[ ] getUrlsFromSearchResult( SearchResponse searchResponse )
{
    return searchResponse.Image.Results
        .Select( x => x.Thumbnail.Url ).ToArray( );
}
```

As an alternative, we can move the conversion to Observable down into the helper method. In that case, the first part is simplified.

```
return observableSearchFunc( searchRequest )
    .SelectMany( response => getUrlsFromSearchResult( response ))
```

And the conversion happens in the helper method.

```
private IObservable<string> getUrlsFromSearchResult( SearchResponse searchResponse )
{
    return searchResponse.Image.Results
        .Select( x => x.Thumbnail.Url ).ToObservable();
}
```

It is important to realize that both ways of doing this have the same end result. The earlier approach is a bit more fluent, but it really is a "fielder's choice."

Since we're only interested in the thumbnail URLs, we use LINQ to select only the ones that we want.

Your project will now build, but it won't do much, not least of which is because we've not implemented an event handler for the search button.

Add an Event Handler for the Search Button

The button event handler in this case will be implemented as a Subject created within the MainWindow constructor.

```
Subject<RoutedEventArgs> clickObservable = new Subject<RoutedEventArgs>( );
SearchButton.Click += ( o, e ) => clickObservable.OnNext( e );
```

A Subject is very much an Observable except for the following two key differences:

1. It is also an Observer; it can both observe and be observed.

2. You can programmatically affect the subject. That is, you can make a method call that will make the contents of the subject available to any observer. You can manually publish the contents one at a time by calling OnNext, for example, and all the subscribers will receive the items each time you do.

The first line creates a Subject of RoutedEventArgs named clickObserverable and assigns to that a new, empty Subject. The second registers an event handler with the Click event on the button, but rather than passing in a traditional event handler, it passes in the OnNext method of the just-created subject.

We can wire up the event handler to pick up the string in the search box and write the text to the output window, again within the constructor, as follows:

```
IObservable<string> searchTermObservable = clickObservable
    .Select( args => SearchBox.Text )
    .Where( term => String.IsNullOrWhiteSpace( term ) == false );

searchTermObservable.Subscribe( term => Console.WriteLine( @"Search for '{0}'", term) );
```

The first line assigns to a new IObservable (searchTermObservable), the clickObservable, selecting the SearchBox Text property where the string is not null or whitespace. The second line then subscribes to that IObservable, passing the string to Console.WriteLine, which writes to the output window.

What we are actually doing here is converting a stream of clicks into a stream of search terms. We are then instructing the Observable to notify us only when that search term is not empty.

A key point here is that we're able to assemble the event we *want* from the events we have. We *want* the event "the user wants to search for something"—what we have is a simple event (a click) and the more useful information of the search term. Reactive Extensions allows us to combine these primitives into a higher-level abstraction: the event we care about.

Implement Rx-based CreateIUmagefromURL

Let's modify the subscribe line to search instead for an image based on the text typed into the search box. To do this, we'll need a member variable of type ObservableCollection<BitmapImage> that we can use as the collection of images we wish to display.

Begin by adding the member variable, as follows:

```
public ObservableCollection<BitmapImage> ImagesToDisplay { get; protected set; }
```

Initialize that member variable in the constructor, as follows:

```
ImagesToDisplay = new ObservableCollection<BitmapImage>( );
```

Update the Subscribe method to clear the collection in preparation for the search, as follows:

```
searchTermObservable.Subscribe (term =>
{
    Console.WriteLine( "Search for '{0}'", term );
    ImagesToDisplay.Clear( );
} );
```

Create from image takes a Url and returns a BitmapImage from that Url, as follows:

```
private BitmapImage createImageFromUrl( string url )
{
    return new BitmapImage  (new Uri(url));
}
```

We are now ready to wire up the search box observable to actually add the image (once again, place this in the constructor), as follows:

```
IObservable<BitmapImage> bitmapImagesToAdd = searchTermObservable
.SelectMany( term => searchBingImageApi( term ) )
.ObserveOnDispatcher( )
.Select( url => createImageFromUrl( url ) );

bitmapImagesToAdd.Subscribe( image => ImagesToDisplay.Add( image ) );
```

As noted in previous chapters, `ObserveOnDispatcher` is used to force execution on the UI thread.

We can now go back to the XAML and wire up the list box, setting the templates in the Resources section. Here's the modified XAML; note the addition of the name `Window` for the main Window, as shown in Listing 4-6.

Listing 4-6. *The modified XAML file for BingImageSearchDemo*

```
<Window
    x:Class="BingImageSearchDemo.MainWindow"
    xmlns="http://schemas.microsoft.com/winfx/2006/xaml/presentation"
    xmlns:x="http://schemas.microsoft.com/winfx/2006/xaml"
    x:Name="Window"
    Title="MainWindow"
    Height="350"
    Width="525">

    <Window.Resources>
        <ItemsPanelTemplate
            x:Key="ItemsPanelTemplate">
            <WrapPanel
                Orientation="Horizontal"
                IsItemsHost="True" />
        </ItemsPanelTemplate>

        <DataTemplate
            x:Key="DataTemplate">
            <Image
                Source="{Binding}"
                Width="128"
                Height="128"
                Margin="8" />
        </DataTemplate>
    </Window.Resources>
```

```
<Grid
    Margin="16">

    <Grid.RowDefinitions>
        <RowDefinition
            Height="Auto" />
        <RowDefinition
            Height="*" />
    </Grid.RowDefinitions>

    <Grid.ColumnDefinitions>
        <ColumnDefinition
            Width="*" />
        <ColumnDefinition
            Width="Auto" />
    </Grid.ColumnDefinitions>

    <TextBox
        x:Name="SearchBox" />

    <Button
        x:Name="SearchButton"
        Grid.Column="1"
        Content="Search"
        Margin="8,0,0,0"
        Width="50" />

    <ListBox
        x:Name="Results"
        Grid.Row="1"
        Grid.ColumnSpan="2"
        Margin="0,8,0,0"
        ScrollViewer.HorizontalScrollBarVisibility="Disabled"
        ItemsSource="{Binding ImagesToDisplay, ElementName=Window}"
        ItemsPanel="{DynamicResource ItemsPanelTemplate}"
        ItemTemplate="{DynamicResource DataTemplate}" />

</Grid>
</Window>
```

The other significant changes are the replacement of the ListBox stub with a Listbox that binds its ItemsSource, ItemsPanel, and ItemsTemplate and the creation of the ItemsPanelTemplate and the DataTemplate resources.

Listing 4-7 is the complete source code for the code-behind file MainWindow.xaml.cs, for context

Listing 4-7. *MainWindow.xaml.cs for BingImageSearchDemo*

```
using System;
using System.Collections.Generic;
using System.Collections.ObjectModel;
using System.Linq;
using System.Reactive.Concurrency;
```

```csharp
using System.Reactive.Linq;
using System.Reactive.Subjects;
using System.Windows;
using System.Windows.Media.Imaging;
using BingImageSearchDemo.BingSearch;

namespace BingImageSearchDemo
{
    public partial class MainWindow : Window
    {
        public ObservableCollection<BitmapImage> ImagesToDisplay { get; protected set; }

        public MainWindow( )
        {
            ImagesToDisplay = new ObservableCollection<BitmapImage>( );
            InitializeComponent( );

            Subject<RoutedEventArgs> clickObservable = new Subject<RoutedEventArgs>( );
            SearchButton.Click += ( o, e ) => clickObservable.OnNext( e );

            IObservable<string> searchTermObservable = clickObservable
                .Select( args => SearchBox.Text )
                .Where( term => String.IsNullOrWhiteSpace( term ) == false );

            searchTermObservable.Subscribe( term =>
            {
                Console.WriteLine( "Search for '{0}'", term );
                ImagesToDisplay.Clear( );
            } );

            IObservable<BitmapImage> bitmapImagesToAdd = searchTermObservable
            .SelectMany( term => searchBingImageApi( term ) )
            .ObserveOnDispatcher()
            .Select( url => createImageFromUrl( url ) );

            bitmapImagesToAdd.Subscribe( image => ImagesToDisplay.Add( image ) );
        }

        private IObservable<string> searchBingImageApi( string query )
        {
            SearchRequest searchRequest = new SearchRequest( );
            searchRequest.AppId = App.BingSearchKey;
            searchRequest.Query = query;
            searchRequest.Sources = new SourceType[ 1 ];
            searchRequest.Sources[ 0 ] = SourceType.Image;

            BingPortTypeClient client = new BingPortTypeClient( );

            Func<SearchRequest, IObservable<SearchResponse>> observableSearchFunc =
                    Observable.FromAsyncPattern<SearchRequest, SearchResponse>(
                            client.BeginSearch, client.EndSearch );
```

```
        return observableSearchFunc( searchRequest )
            .SelectMany( response => getUrlsFromSearchResult( response ).ToObservable( ) );
    }

    private string[ ] getUrlsFromSearchResult( SearchResponse searchResponse )
    {
        return searchResponse.Image.Results.Select( x => x.Thumbnail.Url ).ToArray( );
    }

    private BitmapImage createImageFromUrl( string url )
    {
        return new BitmapImage( new Uri( url ) );
    }
  }
}
```

This program has demonstrated a real-world application of the **FromAsyncPattern** method, showing how Rx can greatly simplify the use of asynchronous methods in your application.

Comparing the Traditional Begin/End approach to Rx.Net

We have asserted that the Rx example shown in Listing 4-7 is easier to maintain than a more traditional (non-Rx) approach. Let's dive a bit deeper into the differences between classic Begin/End asynchronous programming and Rx.

Were it not for Rx, the **searchBingImageApi** method would take a second parameter: a delegate for a callback method.

```
private void searchBingImageApi(string query, Action<string[]> callback)
```

The body of the method would set up the search...

```
SearchRequest searchRequest = new SearchRequest();
searchRequest.AppId = App.BingSearchKey;
searchRequest.Query = query;
searchRequest.Sources = new SourceType[1];
searchRequest.Sources[0] = SourceType.Image;
```

...and then would call **BeginSearch**. As is common with the Begin/End pattern, the method takes three parameters, as follows:

- A **SearchRequest** (the parameters)

- A callback

- An **AsyncState** object

For the first, we'll pass an inline method; for the second, we'll invoke the callback passed in as a parameter; and for the third, we'll pass null.

```
client.BeginSearch(searchRequest, (asyncResult) => {
    var result = client.EndSearch(asyncResult);
    callback(getUrlsFromSearchResult(result));
}, null);
```

When this method completes, it will call getUrlsFromSearchResult, passing in the SearchResponse.

There is only one Begin/End callback in this demonstration program, and we've gone out of our way to flatten the flow of control, but there is no doubt that it is hard to see the linear, step-by-step progression of the program, and is, thus, relatively hard to maintain. Further, when you get to programs that have callbacks calling other methods asynchronously, the flow of control can rapidly become unmanageable.

Listing 4-8, for completeness, and most important, for comparison with the Rx alternative to follow, is the complete source for MainWindow.xaml.cs:

Listing 4-8. *MainWindow.xaml.cs without Rx for BingImageSearchDemo*

```
using System;
using System.Collections.ObjectModel;
using System.Linq;
using System.Windows;
using System.Windows.Media.Imaging;
using BingImageSearchDemo.BingSearch;

namespace BingImageSearchDemo
{
    /// <summary>
    /// Interaction logic for MainWindow.xaml
    /// </summary>
    public partial class MainWindow : Window
    {
        public ObservableCollection<BitmapImage> ImagesToDisplay { get; protected set; }

        public MainWindow()
        {
            ImagesToDisplay = new ObservableCollection<BitmapImage>();

            InitializeComponent();

            SearchButton.Click += (o, e) => {
                if (String.IsNullOrWhiteSpace(SearchBox.Text)) {
                    return;
                }

                Console.WriteLine("Search for '{0}'", SearchBox.Text);
                ImagesToDisplay.Clear();

                searchBingImageApi(SearchBox.Text, (results) => {
                    Dispatcher.BeginInvoke(new Action(() => {
                        foreach(var v in results) {
                            ImagesToDisplay.Add(createImageFromUrl(v));
                        }
                    }));
                });
            };
        }
```

```
    private void searchBingImageApi(string query, Action<string[]> callback)
    {
        SearchRequest searchRequest = new SearchRequest();
        searchRequest.AppId = App.BingSearchKey;
        searchRequest.Query = query;
        searchRequest.Sources = new SourceType[1];
        searchRequest.Sources[0] = SourceType.Image;

        BingPortTypeClient client = new BingPortTypeClient();

        client.BeginSearch(searchRequest, (asyncResult) => {
            var result = client.EndSearch(asyncResult);
            callback(getUrlsFromSearchResult(result));
        }, null);
    }

    private string[] getUrlsFromSearchResult(SearchResponse searchResponse)
    {
        // We're really only interested in the Image thumbnail URLs
        return searchResponse.Image.Results.Select(x => x.Thumbnail.Url).ToArray();
    }

    private BitmapImage createImageFromUrl(string url)
    {
        return new BitmapImage(new Uri(url));
    }
    }
}
```

Comparing the asynchronous (Begin/End) approach with the Rx approach helps you readily see that the latter is far easier to maintain over time. If the traditional asynchronous approach were to add a call to another asynchronous method from within its callback method, the flow of the program would quickly become unintelligible, but the Rx approach would handle that with aplomb.

Summary

In this chapter we looked at some of the more advanced operators and then dug deep into a more extensive example.

We began with a discussion of asynchronous techniques and ended with a full demonstration of a working asynchronous Rx program, in which we built and dissected an application to retrieve images from Bing, based on a select set of keywords using Reactive Extensions.

C H A P T E R 5

Inside Rx

As you've seen in previous chapters, Observables are the heart and soul of Rx. Operators in Rx are extension methods on `IObservable`. In this chapter, we will examine some of the more advanced operators and how they can help you solve various programming problems.

We'll begin by looking at the Window and Buffer operators, with a special emphasis on the core Window (overloaded) operator. We'll then take a look at the Join pattern operators that allow you to subscribe to complex clustering of observables, move on to the Publish and Multicast operators, and discuss how you might implement your own operators. We'll also examine the implicit contract imposed by all Observables and we'll end with a discussion of Schedulers.

Window and Buffer

Frequently you will need to cut an input stream into samples or groups. Rx Windows allow you to do this based on any number of criteria. For example, given a stream of failed logins, determine whether five logins have failed within a three-minute window.

The Window method is used to cut your input stream into segments called (surprise!) Windows, such that each Window has a start and an end. For example, you might have Windows such as "from 3 p.m. to 4 p.m." and "from 4 p.m. to 5 p.m." or you might have a Window such as "from when they click the button until they let go." A very simple example of Windows would be to cut the stream into groups of four items each (start is an empty window and end is when we've seen four items).

The Window method returns an `IObservable<IObservable<T>>`—an `IObservable` of `IObservable` of T —or more conceptually, a future list of future lists. The outer `IObservable` represents a list of `Windows`. Each item in the collection (the inner `IObservable`) is a list of items that happened in the `Window`.

If you don't care about the timing (event arrival) of the items in each window you can use the simpler (but less powerful) alternative: `Buffer`, which returns an `IObservable<List<T>>`. That is, an `Observable` of `Lists`, where the `List` is a collection of the `Items` that fell into each window.

Let's start with the simplest `Buffer` we can create, one which divides a stream of four integers into two lists of two items each.

```
var input = new[] {1,2,3,4,5}.ToObservable();

// Split the input into pieces, with a buffer size of two
int i = 0;
input.Buffer(2).Subscribe(list => {
    // We've got the items, but we've lost the timings of when they happened
    // since list is just a simple IList
```

```
      list.Dump(String.Format("List {0}", ++i));
});
```

If you copy this code snippet into LINQPad, the result shows that your stream has in fact been divided into lists, each of which has two items, as shown in Figure 5-1.

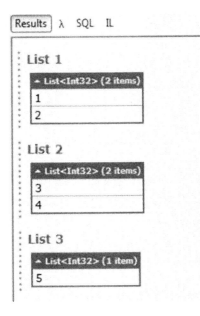

Figure 5-1. *LINQPad Output*

For comparison, let's change the `Buffer` in the snippet to a `Window`, as follows, and run it again:

```
var input = new[] {1,2,3,4,5}.ToObservable();

int i = 0;

// Subscribe to an Observable of Observables
input.Window(2).Subscribe(obs =>
{
  int current = ++i;
  Console.WriteLine("Started Observable {0}", current);

  // Subscribe to the inner Observable and print its items
  obs.Subscribe(
    item => Console.WriteLine("   {0}", item),
    () => Console.WriteLine("Ended Observable {0}", current));
});
```

The console output shows the `Windows` and their contents.

```
Started Observable 1
1
2
Ended Observable 1
Started Observable 2
3
4
Ended Observable 2
Started Observable 3
5
Ended Observable 3
```

There are many types of Window methods, but all derive from the base Window method, as we'll see next.

Understanding Window: The Core Method

All of the Window and Buffer methods inherit from the Window method, which looks like the following:

```
public IObservable<IObservable<T>> Window(
        this IObservable<T> source,
        IObservable<TWindowOpening> windowOpenings,
        Func<TWindowOpening, IObservable<TWindowClosing>> windowClosingSelector);
```

The Window method takes three parameters. The first is a source. The second is an Observable that fires when the Windows should open. The third is a Func that, given an open Window will determine when that Window should close.

The Rx framework provides nine overloads of Window and there are ten Buffer implementations (Buffer derives from Window). This is an extraordinarily flexible method; it is used to implement all of the different scenarios covered by the overloads.

The following is an example that uses the core Window method. Note that in this example we use time to determine the shape of the windows, but we could use *any* IObservable.

```
var sched = new TestScheduler();

var input = sched.CreateColdObservable(
  sched.OnNextAt(205, 1),
  sched.OnNextAt(305, 10),
  sched.OnNextAt(405, 100),
  sched.OnNextAt(505, 1000),
  sched.OnNextAt(605, 10000),
  sched.OnCompletedAt<int>(1100.0));

int i = 0;
var windows = input.Window(
    // We're going to start a window every 100 milliseconds..
    Observable.Timer(TimeSpan.Zero, TimeSpan.FromMilliseconds(100), sched).Take(7),
    // ..and then close it 50ms later.
    x => Observable.Timer(TimeSpan.FromMilliseconds(50), sched));
```

```
windows
  .Timestamp(sched)
  .Subscribe(obs => {
    int current = ++i;
    Console.WriteLine("Started Observable {0} at {1}ms", current, obs.Timestamp.Millisecond);

    // Subscribe to the inner Observable and print its items
    obs.Value.Subscribe(
        item => Console.WriteLine("     {0} at {1}ms", item, sched.Now.Millisecond),
() => Console.WriteLine("Ended Observable {0} at {1}ms\n",
current, sched.Now.Millisecond));
  });
```

The console output should look as follows:

```
sched.Start();
```

```
    Started Observable 1 at 0ms

    Ended Observable 1 at 50ms


    Started Observable 2 at 100ms

    Ended Observable 2 at 150ms


    Started Observable 3 at 200ms

        1 at 205ms

    Ended Observable 3 at 250ms


    Started Observable 4 at 300ms

        10 at 305ms

    Ended Observable 4 at 350ms
```

```
Started Observable 5 at 400ms

    100 at 405ms

Ended Observable 5 at 450ms



Started Observable 6 at 500ms

    1000 at 505ms

Ended Observable 6 at 550ms



Started Observable 7 at 600ms

    10000 at 605ms

Ended Observable 7 at 650ms
```

A second very powerful mechanism for dividing and aggregating objects and data is to apply join operators to your Rx `Observables`, as we'll see in the next section.

Using Join Patterns

Let's take a look at Join pattern operators, which act like Zip on steroids (for a reminder of Zip, see Chapter 5). The Join pattern allows you to combine streams using *And* and *Or*, which lets you match many, more complicated patterns. The typical pattern is "Tell me when either of (A && B && C or D && E) happens. To make this work you'll need to use three main methods, `When`, `And` and `Then`.

- `When()`: At the very end says "Tell me when any of the patterns happen"

- `And()`: Creates a Join pattern by saying "Wait until A *and* B produce an item. These can be concatenated, allowing you to wait for A *and* B *and* C.

- `Then()`: Once you finish combining using *and, then* works like *select*, it allows you to combine the results into a value.

The following example will make this much clearer:

```
var sched = new TestScheduler();

var lhs = sched.CreateColdObservable(
  sched.OnNextAt(200, 1),
  sched.OnNextAt(300, 10),
  sched.OnNextAt(400, 100),
  sched.OnNextAt(500, 1000),
```

```
    sched.OnNextAt(600, 10000),
    sched.OnCompletedAt<int>(1100.0));

var rhs = sched.CreateColdObservable(
  sched.OnNextAt(250, "A"),
  sched.OnNextAt(650, "B"),
  sched.OnNextAt(850, "C"),
  sched.OnCompletedAt<string>(1000));

var join = Observable.When(
  lhs.And(rhs).Then((l,r) => String.Format("{0}:{1}", l,r))
);

join.Timestamp(sched)
  .Select(x => new { Time = x.Timestamp.Millisecond, x.Value })
  .Dump();

sched.Start();
```

The output looks as follows:

```
Time = 250 Value = 1:A

Time = 650 Value = 10:B

Time = 850 Value = 100:C
```

We can easily add a third value and join all three together, as shown in the following code example:

```
var sched = new TestScheduler();

var lhs = sched.CreateColdObservable(
  sched.OnNextAt(200, 1),
  sched.OnNextAt(300, 10),
  sched.OnNextAt(400, 100),
  sched.OnNextAt(500, 1000),
  sched.OnNextAt(600, 10000),
  sched.OnCompletedAt<int>(1100.0));

var rhs = sched.CreateColdObservable(
  sched.OnNextAt(250, "A"),
  sched.OnNextAt(650, "B"),
  sched.OnNextAt(850, "C"),
  sched.OnCompletedAt<string>(1000));

var trigger = sched.CreateColdObservable(
  sched.OnNextAt(900, 4.4),
  sched.OnCompletedAt<double>(901));
```

```
var join = Observable.When(
  lhs.And(rhs).And(trigger).Then((l,r,t) => String.Format("{0}:{1}:{2}", l,r,t))
);

join.Timestamp(sched)
  .Select(x => new { Time = x.Timestamp.Millisecond, x.Value })
  .Dump();

sched.Start();
```

In this example, we create a three-way *And*. Just as with *Zip* we need an item to fill all three slots. Since the third stream only produces an item at 900ms, we will only get one result, at 900ms.

In the next section, we'll look at how using Rx operators can cause side effects, and how the Multicast and Publish operators can mitigate that problem.

Using Multicast, Publish and IConnectableObservable

Rx operators do not themselves have side effects, but at times, using an Rx object will have a side effect. For example, if we create an IObservable with a COM object, when we subscribe we may add a COM addref, and when we unsubscribe we might end up releasing that COM object. Worse, the effect is different if we have two subscribers than if we have one.

This problem can be eliminated using the Multicast and Publish methods. These methods return a a Connectable Observable that shares a subscription to the underlying source.

The following example demonstrates how side effects can sneak into even a simple program. It uses a Hot Observable (remember, that's a single event-stream), with explicit, subscription side effects added via Do(). This is often a place where programmers first encounter overt side effects. A programmer might use Do to print log messages, but then finds that the log messages are duplicated or triplicated as Do is called for each subscription.

```
var sched = new TestScheduler();

var input = sched.CreateHotObservable(
  sched.OnNextAt(200, 1),
  sched.OnNextAt(300, 10),
  sched.OnNextAt(400, 100),
  sched.OnCompletedAt<int>(1100.0));

var sideEffected = input.Do(x => Console.WriteLine("Effects!"));

sideEffected.Subscribe(Console.WriteLine);
sideEffected.Subscribe(Console.WriteLine);
```

When you run this example, you can expect the following output:

Effects!

1

Effects!

1

Effects!

10

Effects!

10

Effects!

100

Effects!

100

Notice that there are two effects for each. Let's add Publish and run the program, we should see that this mitigates the extra side effects because Subscription enables us to have just one subscriber to the source and rebroadcasts the result to all interested subscribers. (Warning! There is no output.)

```
var sched = new TestScheduler();

var input = sched.CreateHotObservable(
    sched.OnNextAt(200, 1),
    sched.OnNextAt(300, 10),
    sched.OnNextAt(400, 100),
    sched.OnCompletedAt<int>(1100.0));

var published = input.Do(x => Console.WriteLine("Effects!")).Publish();

published.Subscribe(Console.WriteLine);
published.Subscribe(Console.WriteLine);

sched.Start();
```

Remember that Publish returns a ConnectableObservable. This allows you to control exactly how many times the side effect happens (typically, you want exactly once). Let's connect to the source (in this case, input) by calling Connect: and see that we get exactly one effect for each iteration.

```
var sched = new TestScheduler();
```

```
var input = sched.CreateHotObservable(
    sched.OnNextAt(200, 1),
    sched.OnNextAt(300, 10),
    sched.OnNextAt(400, 100),
    sched.OnCompletedAt<int>(1100.0));

var published = input.Do(x => Console.WriteLine("Effects!")).Publish();
published.Connect();

published.Subscribe(Console.WriteLine);
published.Subscribe(Console.WriteLine);

sched.Start();
```

The output looks like the following:

```
Effects!

1

1

Effects!

10

10

Effects!

100

100
```

In this output you can see that the *effect* in the "Do" operator was only invoked once per item, rather than twice.

IObservable is the heart and soul of Rx. In the next section, we'll look at the implicit contract offered by IObservable.

Understanding How IObservable Handles OnCompleted and OnError

Let's examine one critical aspect of the contract offered by IObservable: *Once an observable sequence terminates with* OnCompleted *or* OnError, *no more items can be produced.*

This raises the question: how do you get work done if OnCompleted or OnError interrupt the flow with such finality? This section will examine this dilemma and the solution.

The finality of OnCompleted is illustrated in the following example, which schedules a number of values to be observed, but interrupts with OnCompleted after the second value:

```
var sched = new TestScheduler();

var input = sched.CreateColdObservable(
        sched.OnNextAt(200, 1),
        sched.OnNextAt(300, 10),
        sched.OnCompletedAt<int>(350.0),
        sched.OnNextAt(400, 100),
        sched.OnNextAt(500, 1000),
        sched.OnNextAt(600, 10000))
    .AsObservable();

input.Dump();

sched.Start();
```

The output looks as follows:

1

10

Note that after the second value everything grinds to a halt because of receiving OnCompleted.

This aspect of Observable seems quite impractical for those new to Rx, who might ask, "How am I supposed to get anything done when anytime something goes wrong, my entire pipeline is torn down?"

And if every Observable was a Hot Observable, that complaint would be completely correct. However, remember that Cold Observables get a new copy every time someone evaluates them via Subscribe(), First(), or other methods that immediately return a value. This means that Observables that you want to reuse should strive to be Cold Observables. This is the core reason why methods such as Repeat and Retry work—they continually re-subscribe to their input whenever it ends, making the *appearance* of an infinite stream, even when their input ends via an error.

There are a number of methods for managing abrupt termination. Much depends on what you want to do, and Rx forces you to decide. Your choices are

- Make the error disappear?

- Replace the output with a null value?

- Tear everything down?

If you choose to make the error disappear, you can use the Retry method. To follow abort semantics, use the Repeat method. If you want a new Observable every time something bad happens, use the Defer() method, as shown in the next example,

```
int counter = 0;
var input = Observable.Defer(() => {
    // Simulate an Observable that sometimes dies
    if (++counter % 2 == 0) {
        return Observable.Throw<int>(new Exception("Aieeee!"));
    } else {
        return Observable.Return(42);
    }
});

input.Subscribe(x => Console.WriteLine(x), ex => Console.WriteLine(ex.Message));
input.Subscribe(x => Console.WriteLine(x), ex => Console.WriteLine(ex.Message));
input.Subscribe(x => Console.WriteLine(x), ex => Console.WriteLine(ex.Message));
```

The following is the console output you can expect to see:

42

Aieeee!

42

You have seen how the advanced operators of Rx can be applied to various programming problems. There are times, however, when you will wish to create custom operators to meet specific requirements. The next section walks you through the creation of custom extensions to IObservable.

Implementing Your Own Operators

While Rx provides a number of operators to manage even very complex programming situations, there will be times when you need to customize the behavior for your specific goal.

Since operators in both Rx and LINQ are simply extension methods on IObservable and IEnumerable, it's easy to create your own. The simplest way to create your own operators is by combining existing operators.

We'll use Aggregate in a clever way, since it already encapsulates "return a value when the input completes." We'll use the First method to do the blocking for us.

```
public static class BlockingObservableMixins
{
    public static void BlockUntilCompleted<T>(this IObservable<T> input)
    {
        input.Aggregate(0, (acc, x) => acc).First();
    }
}

public static class SelectUsingSelectManyMixin
{
    // Here, we'll re-implement Select using SelectMany - this is also an example
    // of an operator that returns an IObservable, so it can be put in the
```

```
        // middle of a pipeline.
        public static IObservable<TRet> SelectUsingSelectMany<T, TRet>(
                        this IObservable<T> input, Func<T, TRet> selector)
        {
            return input.SelectMany(x =>
                Observable.Return(selector(x)));
        }
}
```

In this example we did not use any manual synchronization, such as `ManualResetEvent`. Using these lock primitives defeats the Rx abstraction, and is a "code smell" (that is, an indication that something is not correct in the code).

While some operators in Rx are implemented using other operators, some operators must be directly implemented. This can be done by implementing `IObservable` yourself, but a better idea is to use `Observable.Create`.

When you create your own operators, you must follow the `Observable` contract, which requires that after you complete, you do not produce any additional items, and that your operators follow Abort semantics. Abort semantics usually require that when any of your inputs `OnError`, you should immediately `OnError` yourself).

Another important aspect of implementing operators directly, is that you must manage `Disposables` properly. Unlike many uses of Rx, you almost always need to handle the result returned by `Subscribe`, since when someone unsubscribes to your operator, you should in-turn unsubscribe to your input. This gets more complicated when you accept more than one `Observable`, like `Merge` or `Concat`—you should always write a spec to describe what your operator should do in different circumstances before you write your code.

To illustrate how you might create your own extension method, the following example shows how you can implement `Where` using `Observable.Create`.

```
public static class WhereUsingObservableCreate
{
    public static IObservable<T> WhereUsingObsCreate<T>(this IObservable<T> input, Func<T,
bool> predicate)
    {
        return Observable.Create<T>(subj => {
            bool finished = false;

            // Subscribe to the input
            IDisposable disconnectInput = input.Subscribe(
                // If we're not finished, and the Where clause matches, pass it
                // on down
                x => if (!finished && predicate(x) == true) { subj.OnNext(x); },

                // If we fail, we're done - pass the error down
                ex => { finished = true; subj.OnError(ex); },

                // If the input completes, we complete too
                () => { finished = true; subj.OnCompleted(); }
            );

            return disconnectInput;
        });
    }
}
```

`Observable.Create` is a bit tricky to wrap your head around—it returns a *cold* `Observable`; whenever someone subscribes, the `Func` you provide it will be called.

You can think of the input parameter as a `Subject` that you get to manually push values to whenever you want—it's an `Observable` that you control by hand.

The return value is also hard to understand. Whenever someone unsubscribes from the subscription, you return an `IDisposable` that is disposed, kind of like a "Destructor" for your new `Observable` (but not like a C++ destructor or a finalizer).

We return a `Disposable` that will be disposed when people unsubscribe to our operator. Sometimes, you don't need anything at all to happen when the operator is unsubscribed, but in this case we want to disconnect our subscription to the input `Observable`.

Many operators care about concurrency, and these operators all interact with Schedulers, the topic of the next section.

Using Schedulers

Operators that care about concurrency will take an `IScheduler` as a parameter. This lets you specify the context in which the operator will run.

Normally, and for most operators in Rx (and in LINQ), you specify what will happen, but not the context in which it will happen. Rx generally frees you from caring. This is very different from traditional imperative programming in which all synchronization is explicit, and you must manage all the elements of asynchronous programming, such as the creation of threads and locks. In traditional programming your code never suddenly runs in a background thread; you make that happen programmatically.

Rx changes that. Every time you write some code that runs in a `Select()` or `Where()` operator, you should say to yourself, "I have no idea what thread this is on."

Rx will happily run on any thread, and many times ends up on a thread that's different than the thread you created the pipeline on. If you only access local variables, or variables passed into your method, this works with no problem. If you write your program in a purely functional way (i.e. you never access variables outside of the method), or if you only use local variables that you know won't be touched by more than one person at a time, this is completely safe.

Rx is free to run your code wherever it wants, which is very powerful—just like in LINQ where you can suddenly add `AsParallel()` and make your code run on extra threads, with no other changes.

However, many components aren't so flexible. If you're using technologies such as WPF, Silverlight, or COM, they may require that objects are only manipulated on certain threads. Or maybe, you are accessing an external resource that can only be used by one person at a time. By default, code is run in context, as in the fastest way to do some work is to just do it immediately.

However, some operators such as `Timer` don't make sense in an immediate context—they need to be deferred. To manipulate where code runs, we can use an `IScheduler`. Operators that have elements of concurrency such as `ForkJoin` or `Timer` will have an `IScheduler` parameter, which lets you specify in which context the `Timer` will run.

Fortunately, the Rx team has already covered most of the cases you are likely to care about, as follows:

- `Scheduler.Immediate`: Run the code immediately, don't schedule.

- `Scheduler.NewThread`: Run the code in a new thread.

- `Scheduler.TaskPool`: Run the code in a TPL Task. (This is usually the one you want.)

- `Scheduler.ThreadPool`: Run the code on the .NET 3.5 ThreadPool

- `Scheduler.CurrentThread`: Like `Immediate`, but resolve dependencies so you don't deadlock yourself .

- `DispatcherScheduler`: **Run the code on the WPF/Silverlight UI thread.**

- `ControlScheduler`: Run the code on the WinForms UI thread.

The following is a code example that illustrates the explicit use of the `Immediate` and `TaskPool` schedulers to manage the thread context.

```
Observable.Range(0, 20, Scheduler.TaskPool).Select(x =>
Thread.CurrentThread.ManagedThreadId).Dump("Taskpool Thread ID");

// Wait so we don't see results coming in from both queries in between each
// other
Thread.Sleep(5 * 1000);

Observable.Range(0, 20, Scheduler.Immediate).Select(x =>
Thread.CurrentThread.ManagedThreadId).Dump("Immediate Thread ID");
```

In this example, we see that the `TaskPool` threads will usually be different for different items. Thus, not all the items will have the same `ThreadID`. On the other hand, when we call `ImmediateThreadID` we always see the same `threadID` for all the items.

Summary

In this chapter we saw how to divide or segment an observable into groups using the core Window operator and its overloads, including the associated Buffer operator. We were able to bring together disparate `Observables` using the Join pattern and we looked at how to manage when `OnCompleted` or `OnError` bring an `Observable` to an abrupt stop.

CHAPTER 6

LINQ to SQL

Within very disparate applications, developers must deal with certain problems that repeatedly arise in programming. One of the most common problems is the need to map objects and their properties to tables and columns in a database.

LINQ to SQL can be used as an object-relational mapping (ORM) framework and bridges this seemingly insurmountable gap. Now that LINQ to SQL has been adopted as the approach for Windows Phone database management, it is at the forefront of Windows Phone development.

Using a database on a phone may initially seem to be a strange thing to do. Surely databases are for large servers! However, the guarantees provided by modern databases for consistency and atomicity make it a useful data storage layer for any application. Furthermore, databases also provide a natural yet performance-optimized language with which to query information.

In this chapter, you will learn how to use LINQ to SQL and you'll see the differences between LINQ to Objects and LINQ to SQL. In addition, you'll learn how to create a data context for LINQ, how to query the database, and how to use joins to merge two or more tables into a single flat virtual table.

While LINQ to SQL for the Windows Phone is not identical to the .NET Framework version, veterans of the desktop framework will find the Windows Phone version familiar, and much of the code written for the desktop will be reusable.

Introducing LINQ to SQL

LINQ to SQL consists of an object model and a runtime. The object model is encapsulated in the *DataContext* object (an object that inherits from System.Data.Linq.DataContext). The runtime mediates between objects (the DataContext) and relational data (the local database).

Before we get down to the details of using LINQ to SQL on the phone, we can familiarize ourselves with the query language of LINQ to SQL via LINQPad. With LINQPad, we can connect to existing databases, and "explore" the data. When writing code to interface with existing databases, this is a great first step, as it will give you a better idea on how to start writing an application.

Fortunately, even if you don't have an existing database, Microsoft has provided several sample databases that are available online, such as the AdventureWorks database and the older Northwind database. These databases contain a schema that models solving a common business problem, such as recording product sales. AdventureWorks and Northwind both also contain sample data, which makes testing queries more straightforward.

Test LINQ to SQL Queries with LINQPad

There are two ways to set up LINQPad to work with the SampleData. The easiest is to open LINQPad, click on the Samples tab (in the lower-left part of the screen), navigate to this book's entry, and install it. As an alternative, you can download the Northwind database from MSDN at `http://msdn.microsoft. com/en-us/library/ms227484%28v=vs.80%29.aspx`, and place it in a known location. You can then click on Add Connection in LINQPad's connection window (in the upper-right part of the screen), click Next, select Attach Database File, and navigate to the file.

Write a Query

The following code shows a simple LINQPad query that tests your connection and also shows a basic LINQ query at work. Try it.

```
DataContext dataContext = this;

IQueryable<Contacts> query = from Contact in dataContext.GetTable<Contacts>()
            select Contact;

query.Dump();
```

Filter Results with a Where Clause

You can restrict both the values searched (using a where clause) and the values returned (by creating an anonymous type with just the values you want). This is illustrated in the following code snippet:

```
DataContext dataContext = this;

var query = from Contact in dataContext.GetTable<Contacts>()
  where Contact.City == "London"
  select new
  {
    Contact.ContactID,
    Contact.CompanyName,
    Contact.ContactName
  };

query.Dump();
```

The where clause where Contact.City == "London" restricts the search to those records whose City column contains the string "London," just as it would do in TSQL. The select new construct restricts which columns are returned from the database to those in the anonymous type created (that is, to the three columns *ContactID*, *CompanyName* and *ContactName*).

The output for this is shown in Figure 6-1.

ContactID	CompanyName	ContactName
4	Around the Horn	Thomas Hardy
11	B's Beverages	Victoria Ashworth
16	Consolidated Holdings	Elizabeth Brown
19	Eastern Connection	Ann Devon
53	North/South	Simon Crowther
72	Seven Seas Imports	Hari Kumar
92	Exotic Liquids	Charlotte Cooper
125	Northwind	Mr. Steven Buchanan
126	Northwind	Mr. Michael Suyama
127	Northwind	Mr. Robert King
129	Northwind	Ms. Anne Dodsworth

IOrderedQueryable<> (11 items)

Figure 6-1. *Output of using the where filter*

Writing LINQ to SQL Code with Visual Studio

It is important to make sure you are comfortable translating these queries from LINQPad back to a program written in Visual Studio. While you can, of course, write these programs in any language that supports LINQ (both in LINQPad and in Visual Studio), this book will use C#.

One difference that is specific to Windows Phone is that we cannot create our database visually using a Visual Studio designer—as you may be accustomed to when writing ASP.NET web sites or Windows applications—nor can you import a schema from an existing SQL Server database. Instead, before you are able to query databases on Windows Phone, you must describe each of our data tables in code using a simple, attribute-based syntax.

To see how to map a LINQPad program to Visual Studio, open Visual Studio, create a new console application, and name it SimplestQuery, for example.

Add LINQ Libraries and Namespaces

Be sure to include the library `System.Data.LINQ` and add the following two `using` statements at the top of each file:

```
using System.Data.Linq;
using System.Data.Linq.Mapping;
```

Create an Entity Class

The very first job is to map the database to an entity; that is, to a class that will represent the table. To do so, create a new class named *Customer* and adorn the class and its properties with attributes, as shown in the following code:

```
[Table(Name="Customers")]
class Customer
{
    [Column( IsPrimaryKey = true )]
    public string CustomerID { get; set; }
```

```
    [Column(Name="ContactName")]
    public string Contact { get; set; }

    [Column(Name="CompanyName")]
    public string Company { get; set; }

    [Column]
    public string City { get; set; }
}
```

You are free to add properties that do not have the *Column* attribute and which do not map to columns in the database; thus allowing your objects to extend the values in the database.

Notice the `Table` attribute has the `Name=` attribute, allowing your class to have a different name than the table. Similarly, the second and third columns use the `Name=` attribute to allow a property to map to a column with a different name. Finally, the first property, `CustomerID`, has the `IsPrimaryKey` attribute set to true; as must be done for at least one property in every LINQ to SQL class.

Create a DataContext

With this class in place, you are ready to create the all-important `DataContext` object and then to use that to query the database and to populate instances of your class.

Open Program.cs and in the constructor, create the `DataContext`, passing in the path to the Northwind database file. It should look like the following:

```
DataContext db = new DataContext( @"L:\Downloads\Northwind\Northwind.mdf" );
```

Note The `DataContext` encapsulates an ADO.Net Connection object that is initialized with the connection string that you supply in the constructor. This and all of ADO.Net is quite well-hidden by.LINQ To SQL

Query the Database

Use that database to retrieve a strongly-typed instance of `Table<Customer>` (the type you created earlier in Customer.cs).

```
Table<Customer> Customers = db.GetTable<Customer>();
```

You can now create your query statement, just as you did in LINQPad, as follows:

```
var CustomerQuery = from c in Customers
                    where c.City == "London"
                    select new
                    {
                        c.CustomerID,
                        c.Company,
                        c.Contact
                    };
```

All that is left is to iterate through the results to show the same output as LINQPad's Dump() method did, as follows:

```
foreach (var cust in CustomerQuery)
{
    Console.WriteLine( "id = {0}, Company = {1}, Contact = {2}", cust.CustomerID,
cust.Company, cust.Contact );
}
```

The following is the output from running this console application:

```
id = AROUT, Company = Around the Horn, Contact = Thomas Hardy
id = BSBEV, Company = B's Beverages, Contact = Victoria Ashworth
id = CONSH, Company = Consolidated Holdings, Contact = Elizabeth Brown
id = EASTC, Company = Eastern Connection, Contact = Ann Devon
id = NORTS, Company = North/South, Contact = Simon Crowther
id = SEVES, Company = Seven Seas Imports, Contact = Hari Kumar
```

You can see that the LINQPad query and the C# query are identical, as are the output from each program. LINQPad offers a fast and easy way to work with LINQ to SQL that can easily be translated back into any program in any language that supports LINQ.

Inspect a SQL Query

The best way to increase the efficiency of your queries is to examine the actual SQL that is being sent to the database. Doing so can uncover the following two classic problems:

- Querying for records you don't need and that can easily be eliminated

- Querying for columns of data you don't need and that can easily be eliminated

You can eliminate records you don't need by using filters (where clauses, etc.) and you can eliminate columns you don't need by projecting the columns you do need in the select statement.

Observing the actual SQL sent back and forth can also identify where you are making two or more calls, where one is possible.

LINQPad allows you to see the actual SQL that will be generated by your query just by clicking on the SQL button in the results pane, as shown in Figure 6-2.

Figure 6-2. LINQPad SQL Window

You can accomplish the same thing, seeing the SQL that is produced, by adding the following line to your program in Visual Studio:

```
Console.WriteLine( db.GetCommand( CustomerQuery ).CommandText );
```

Place this line of code immediately above the **foreach** loop, and the SQL command will be displayed before the values of the matching records.

Understand the *Table<T>* Class

If you hover over the **var** keyword that serves as the type for **CustomerQuery** you will see that its real type is the interface *IQueryable*, as is shown in Figure 6-3.

```
var CustomerQuery = from c in Customers

interface System.Linq.IQueryable<out T>
Provides functionality to evaluate queries against a specific data source wherein the type of the data is known.

T is 'a

Anonymous Types:
  'a is new { string CustomerID, string Company, string Contact }
```

Figure 6-3. *The real type for CustomerQuery*

Table<T> is a LINQ to SQL class that implements *IQueryable*. *IQueryable* extends *IEnumerable* and allows you to work with the strongly-typed generic; that is, in this case an *IQueryable<Customer>*.

Now you have seen how to model our database tables as classes that have the Table attribute, as well as how to create a DataContext. Once you have a DataContext, you're ready to start making queries against the data. Initially, we've only shown very simple queries, but in the next section, we'll see how to write more complex queries involving more than one table, as well as how to summarize data via Aggregate operators such as Max or Count.

Using LINQ to SQL

One of the great things about LINQ to SQL is that the syntax is identical to LINQ to Objects. LINQ to SQL is a powerful demonstration of one of the core concepts of functional programming: the separation of declaration and mechanism. What does that mean? In LINQ, you describe how the desired result is related to the input data using operators. While these operators have a consistent definition of how they will act on data, what they don't do is specify *how* they do the work. Since operators are not tied to a specific implementation, frameworks are free to implement operators in different ways.

In this case, LINQ to SQL will actually take our query and transform it into an internal optimized representation that it will send directly to the SQL engine. Meaning that we can write code in LINQ, and it is transformed by the framework into optimized SQL queries. Let's dive in to using LINQ in the context of LINQ to SQL.

Manipulating Queries with the Take and Skip Operators

Because the query is written with LINQ, you can use all the LINQ operators to manipulate your results. In previous chapters, we've looked at the *Take* and *Skip* operators; you can narrow your results by using these operators in the query, as shown in Listing 6-1.

Listing 6-1. *Using LINQ Operators on Query Results*

```
DataContext dataContext = this;

var query = from Contact in dataContext.GetTable<Contacts>()
  where Contact.City == "London"
  select new
  {
    Contact.ContactID,
    Contact.CompanyName,
    Contact.ContactName
  };

var afterSkipping = query.Skip(2);
var takingTwo = afterSkipping.Take(2);

takingTwo.Dump();
```

The output looks like Figure 6-4.

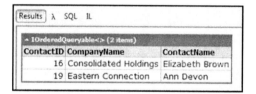

Figure 6-4. *After Skip 2 and Take 2*

Sort and Group Results with the orderby and orderby_descending Operators

Key to the success and value of LINQ to SQL is the ability to let the database do the work that it does best. For example, it is certainly possible to sort the results of a query in C#, but this involves a lot of code and fails to leverage the indices already in the database. A better alternative is to use the query operators orderby and orderby_descending, as shown in Listing 6-2.

Listing 6-2. *Using orderby and orderby_descending*

```
DataContext dataContext = this;

var query = from Contact in dataContext.GetTable<Contacts>()
  where Contact.City == "London"
  orderby Contact.CompanyName
  select new
  {
```

```
      Contact.ContactID,
      Contact.CompanyName,
      Contact.ContactName
   };
query.Dump();
```

Listing 6-3 shows the SQL sent to the database. You can see that the **orderby** operator has been translated to an `ORDER BY` clause, allowing the database to do the sorting.

Listing 6-3. *The SQL Code Generated by Listing 6-2*

```
SELECT [t0].[ContactID], [t0].[CompanyName], [t0].[ContactName]
FROM [Contacts] AS [t0]
WHERE [t0].[City] = @p0
ORDER BY [t0].[CompanyName]
```

Aggregating and Grouping Results with IEnumerable and Its Extensions

The database provides the ability to group results, and *IEnumerable* and its extensions provide an easy way to aggregate and count the members in a group. Let's create an anonymous type that will display the company name and the number of records for each company, as shown in Listing 6-4.

Listing 6-4. *Grouping and Aggregating Query Results*

```
DataContext dataContext = this;

var query = from Contact in dataContext.GetTable<Contacts>()
  where Contact.City == "London"
  group Contact by Contact.CompanyName into Companies
  select new
  {
    Companies.Key,
    count = Companies.Count()
  };
query.Dump();
```

The results of this query are shown in Figure 6-5.

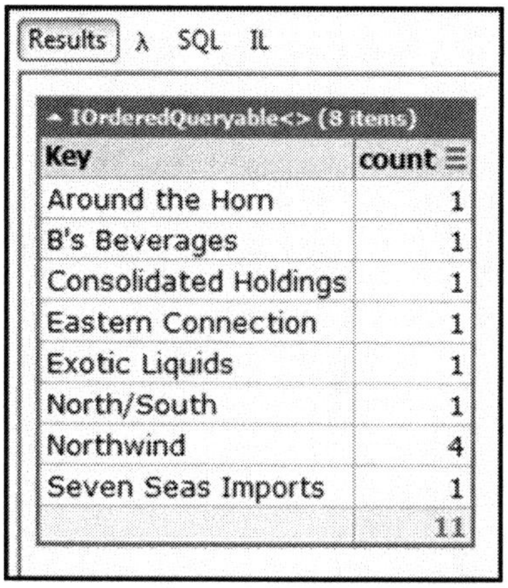

Figure 6-5. *Results of Aggregating and Grouping Query Results*

Nuances of this query can best be understood, again, by looking at the SQL generated, as shown in Listing 6-5.

Listing 6-5. *The SQL Generated by Listing 6-4*

```
SELECT COUNT(*) AS [count], [t0].[CompanyName] AS [Key]
FROM [Contacts] AS [t0]
WHERE [t0].[City] = @p0
GROUP BY [t0].[CompanyName]
```

Notice that the Select statement translates the request for `Companies.Key` to a request for `[CompanyName] AS [Key]`.

This query is very efficient, returning only those parts of those records needed for the output, and letting the database do the processing and counting on our behalf.

Using LINQ to SQL Joins, Cross Joins, and Outer Joins

The heart and soul of a relational database is the normalization of tables so that data is not duplicated (and thus, so that data is less subject to data corruption). A fairly simple example of this can be seen in the *Orders* table of the Northwind database. It would be simple and convenient to put each customer's data (name, address, etc.) into each order, but that would mean that the data for a given customer might be duplicated (perhaps many times over) throughout the *Orders* table.

What is done, instead, is to create a single record for each Customer in the *Customers* table, giving each record a unique ID (`CustomerID`). That ID is then used as a foreign key in the Orders table, allowing each order to unambiguously identify the associated customer.

When it is time to retrieve data about a given order (such as the order date, the customer's company name and the customer's postal code) the two tables are *joined* on the `CustomerID`. This can be done in LINQ to SQL using the *join* operator, as shown in Listing 6-6.

Listing 6-6. *Joining the Order and Customer tables*

```
DataContext dataContext = this;

var orders = dataContext.GetTable<Orders>();
var customers = dataContext.GetTable<Customers>();

var query = from order in orders join customer in customers
on order.CustomerID equals customer.CustomerID
select new
{
  order.OrderDate,
  customer.CompanyName,
  customer.PostalCode
};
```

```
query.Dump();
```

An excerpt from results of this query are shown in Figure 6-6.

OrderDate	CompanyName	PostalCode
7/4/1996 12:00:00 AM	Vins et alcools Chevalier	51100
7/5/1996 12:00:00 AM	Toms Spezialitäten	44087
7/8/1996 12:00:00 AM	Hanari Carnes	05454-876
7/8/1996 12:00:00 AM	Victuailles en stock	69004
7/9/1996 12:00:00 AM	Suprêmes délices	B-6000
7/10/1996 12:00:00 AM	Hanari Carnes	05454-876
7/11/1996 12:00:00 AM	Chop-suey Chinese	3012
7/12/1996 12:00:00 AM	Richter Supermarkt	1203
7/15/1996 12:00:00 AM	Wellington Importadora	08737-363

Figure 6-6. *Excerpt of output from join*

The *join* shown above is a *cross join*. Records will only be returned when there is a matching row in both the order and the Customer class. You may, at times, wish to write an *outer join*, in which you will return records whether or not there is a matching customer record. To do this, you create the original join and then invoke the `DefaultIfEmpty()` method on that new object, as shown in Listing 6-7.

Listing 6-7. *Outer Join*

```
var customers = dataContext.GetTable<Customers>();
var orders = dataContext.GetTable<Orders>();

var query = from order in orders join customer in customers
on order.CustomerID equals customer.CustomerID into customersOrders
```

```
from customerOrder in customersOrders.DefaultIfEmpty()
select new
{
  order.OrderDate,
  customerOrder.CompanyName,
  customerOrder.PostalCode
};
```

Using LINQ to SQL to Work with Relationships

Objects are typically not isolated entities; they exist in relationship to other objects. The three principle relationships in object oriented programming are *is-a, has-a,* and *relates-to*. The first is modeled through inheritance, the second through composition, and the third through method calls.

Not surprisingly, the heart of relational databases is relations; in this case, modeled by foreign key relationships.

Mapping from object relationships to relational database relationships is the main objective of LINQ to SQL.

We can model the relationship between the Customer class and the Order class more explicitly by the use of attributes in both classes. For example, we can mark up the Customer class as shown in Listing 6-8.

Listing 6-8. Customer Class with EntitySet

```
[Table(Name="Customers")]
 class Customer
 {
     [Column( IsPrimaryKey = true )]
     public string CustomerID { get; set; }

     [Column]
     public string CompanyName { get; set; }

     [Column]
     public string ContactName { get; set; }

     [Column]
     public string City { get; set; }

     private EntitySet<Order> _orders;

     [Association( Storage = "_orders", OtherKey = "CustomerID" )]
     public EntitySet<Order> Orders
     {
         get { return this._orders; }
         set { _orders.Assign( value ); }
     }
}
```

Notice especially the EntitySet type on the private member variable _orders and the return type of EntitySet on the *Orders* property, which uses the member variable as its storage. The second attribute on the association attribute for *Orders* is *OtherKey*, which refers to the foreign key in the *Orders* table. This relationship is mirrored in the *Orders* class, as shown in Listing 6-9.

Listing 6-9. *The Orders Table With EntityRef*

```
[Table(Name="Orders")]
class Order
{
    [Column( IsPrimaryKey = true )]
    public int OrderID;

    [Column]
    public string CustomerID;

    private EntityRef<Customer> _customer;

    [Association( Storage = "_customer", ThisKey = "CustomerID" )]
    public Customer Customer
    {
        get { return this._customer.Entity; }
        set { this._customer.Entity = value; }
    }
}
```

This class has an EntityRef because the relationship is one:many, that is each order has one Customer, but any Customer may have many orders. With these relationships in place, we can create a query to find all the orders for each customer, as shown in Listing 6-10.

Listing 6-10. *Finding All the Orders for Each Customer*

```
static void Main( string[ ] args )
{
    var db = new NorthWndDataContext( "L: \\NORTHWND.mdf" );
    var q = from cust in db.Customers
            from ord in db.Orders
            select new
            {
                cust.CustomerID,
                cust.City,
                ord.OrderID
            };

    foreach (var record in q)
    {
        Console.WriteLine( record );
    }
}
```

An excerpt of the output is shown in Listing 6-11.

Listing 6-11. An Excerpt from the Output of the Search Shown in Listing 6-10

```
{ CustomerID = BOLID, City = Madrid, OrderID = 10458 }

{ CustomerID = BOLID, City = Madrid, OrderID = 10461 }

{ CustomerID = BOLID, City = Madrid, OrderID = 10463 }

{ CustomerID = BOLID, City = Madrid, OrderID = 10465 }

{ CustomerID = ANATR, City = México D.F., OrderID = 10282 }

{ CustomerID = ANATR, City = México D.F., OrderID = 10284 }
```

Note that for this to work, we had to create the NorthWndDataContext, as shown in the following statement:

```
class NorthWndDataContext : DataContext
{
    public Table<Customer> Customers;
    public Table<Order> Orders;
    public NorthWndDataContext( string connection ) :
        base( connection ) { }
}
```

Example: Building a Windows Phone Application Using LINQ to SQL

While LINQ to SQL can be used in every aspect of .NET programming, it is particularly crucial in Windows Phone programming where creating a database on top of isolated storage depends on LINQ to SQL.

Let's return to Visual Studio and create a new Windows Phone application that creates a database of Books and their Publishers. Key to this exercise is that each book has a publisher, an object-oriented relationship that we want LINQ to SQL to map to the relational relationship in SQL Server (CE).

Let's begin by creating a new Windows Phone application. It is important to point out that you must have the Windows Phone 7.1 SDK or later installed, since LINQ to SQL was not included in the original release of Windows Phone.

On Main.xaml add two rows and place a button control in each. Name the first one CreateBooks and set its contents to Create Books. Similarly, name the second button ShowBooks and set its contents to Show Books.

Create the Entity Classes

We will have a Book class and a Publisher class. **The relationship is one-to-many** (each book has one publisher, but any publisher may have many books).

Be sure to add a reference to System.Data.LINQ and to add the two necessary using statements in each file, as follows:

```
using System.Data.Linq.Mapping;
using System.Data.Linq;
```

Let's begin by creating the Publisher class, as shown in Listing 6-12.

Listing 6-12. The Publisher Class

```
[Table]
 public class Publisher
 {
     [Column( IsPrimaryKey = true )]
     public string PublisherID { get; set; }

     [Column]
     public string Name { get; set; }

     [Column]
     public string City { get; set; }

     [Column]
     public string Url { get; set; }
 }
```

We also need an Author class, shown in its simplest form in Listing 6-13.

Listing 6-13. Author Class

```
    [Table]
    class Author
    {
        [Column( IsPrimaryKey=true)]
        public int AuthorID { get; set; }

        [Column]
        public int Name { get; set; }
    }
```

We next turn to creating the Book class, as shown in Listing 6-14, which needs to be able to identify the associated publisher through the Publisher ID.

Listing 6-14. The Book Class

```
    [Table]
    public class Book
    {
        [Column( IsPrimaryKey = true )]
        public string BookID { get; set; }
```

```
[Column]
public string Title { get; set; }

[Column]
public string PublisherID { get; set; }

private EntityRef<Publisher> _publisher;

[Association(
    OtherKey = "PublisherID",
    ThisKey = "PublisherID",
    Storage = "_publisher" )]
public Publisher BookPublisher
{
    get
    {
        return _publisher.Entity;
    }
    set
    {
        _publisher.Entity = value;
        PublisherID = value.PublisherID;
    }
}

[Column]
public DateTime PublicationDate { get; set; }

}
```

We have a public *PublisherID,* which allows us to link this Book's publisher to the ID of a publisher in the database. In addition, we have a private *Entity Reference* back to the instance of the Publisher class. Finally, we add the public property *BookPublisher,* adorning it with the Association attribute. In this case we've added three properties to the attribute:

- OtherKey: The key as it is represented in the Publisher class

- ThisKey: The foreign key in the Book class

- Storage: The backing variable for the property

Define the DataContext

We begin the work of managing the data by creating a Data Context, which is an object that derives from DataContext and identifies the tables associated with each object, as shown in Listing 6-15.

Listing 6-15. The BooksDataContext

```
public class BooksDataContext : DataContext
{
    public Table<Book> Books;
```

```
    public Table<Author> Authors;
    public Table<Publisher> Publishers;
    public BooksDataContext(string connection) :
        base(connection) {}
}
```

Instantiate the DataContext

Turn to the code behind file MainPage.xaml.cs and in the constructor create an instance of the BooksDataContext. Note that if it already exists, we delete it and re-create it.

```
DataContext db =
    new BooksDataContext( "isostore:/bookDB.sdf" );
if (db.DatabaseExists())
    db.DeleteDatabase();
db.CreateDatabase();
```

Also set up the event handlers for the two buttons. For context, Listing 6-16 shows the complete constructor.

Listing 6-16. *The Complete Constructor*

```
public MainPage()
{
    InitializeComponent();
    DataContext db =
        new BooksDataContext( "isostore:/bookDB.sdf" );
    if (!db.DatabaseExists())
        db.CreateDatabase();

    CreateBooks.Click +=
      new RoutedEventHandler( CreateBook_Click );
    ShowBooks.Click +=
      new RoutedEventHandler( ShowData_Click );
}
```

Write the CreateBooks Event Handler

The heart of the work is done in the CreateBooks event handler. In Listing 6-17 you will instantiate a couple publishers, as first shown in Listing 6-16.

Listing 6-17. *The Publisher Instances*

```
BooksDataContext db =
    new BooksDataContext( "isostore:/bookDB.sdf" );
```

```
Publisher pub = new Publisher()
{
    PublisherID = "1",
    Name = "Apress",
    City = "Acton",
    Url = "http://Apress.com"
};
db.Publishers.InsertOnSubmit( pub );

Publisher pub2 = new Publisher()
{
    PublisherID = "2",
    Name = "O'Reilly",
    City = "Cambridge",
    Url = "http://Oreilly.com"
};
db.Publishers.InsertOnSubmit( pub2 );
```

Note that the event handler first retrieves a reference to the same BooksDataContext created in the constructor. This ensures that all the methods are talking to the same database instance. After you create the Publishers, you are ready to create a few Book instances. Each Book instance will have a Publisher. This *has-a* relationship will be mapped by LINQ to SQL to the primary keys and foreign keys of a relational database. The creation of the Books is shown in Listing 6-18.

Listing 6-18. Creating Book Instances

```
Book theBook = new Book()
{
    BookID = "1",
    BookPublisher = pub,
    PublicationDate = DateTime.Now,
    Title = "Programming Reactive Extensions"
};
db.Books.InsertOnSubmit( theBook );

theBook = new Book()
{
    BookID = "2",
    BookPublisher = pub,
    PublicationDate = DateTime.Now,
    Title="Migrating to Windows Phone"
};
db.Books.InsertOnSubmit( theBook );

theBook = new Book()
{
    BookID = "3",
    BookPublisher = pub2,
    PublicationDate = DateTime.Now,
    Title = "Programming C#"
};
db.Books.InsertOnSubmit( theBook );
```

Create the UI

When we are ready to display the Books, **we will execute a query obtaining the Books, ordered by Title.** We can then assign the results to the ItemsSource property of a ListBox that we'll add to the third row of MainPage.xaml, as shown in Listing 6-19.

Listing 6-19. The ListBox

```
<ListBox
    Name="BooksLB"
    Grid.Row="2"
    VerticalAlignment="Stretch"
    HorizontalAlignment="Stretch"
    Margin="20">
<ListBox.ItemTemplate>
    <DataTemplate>
        <StackPanel>
            <TextBlock
                Text="{Binding Title}" />
            <StackPanel
                Orientation="Horizontal">
                <TextBlock
                    Text="Publisher: " />
                <TextBlock
                    Text="{ Binding Path=BookPublisher.Name}" />
            </StackPanel>
            <StackPanel
                Orientation="Horizontal">
                <TextBlock
                    Text="Published: " />
                <TextBlock
                    Text="{Binding PublicationDate}" />
            </StackPanel>
            <TextBlock
                Text="-----------------" />
        </StackPanel>
    </DataTemplate>
</ListBox.ItemTemplate>
</ListBox>
```

The essence of this markup is that each ListBox item will be bound to and will display three properties of each Book in the collection it is given as its ItemsSource: the title, the publisher's name, and the publication date.

Write the LINQ Queries

The query itself is shown in Listing 6-19.

```
var q = from b in db.Books
        orderby b.Title
        select b;

BooksLB.ItemsSource = q;
```

As noted earlier, it is more efficient to restrict the columns retrieved by projecting the results into the required Properties in the select statement, as shown in Listing 6-20.

Listing 6-20. The LINQ Query Projecting the Required Properties

```
var q = from b in db.Books
        orderby b.Title
        select new
        {
            b.Title,
            b.PublicationDate,
            b.BookPublisher
        };

BooksLB.ItemsSource = q;
```

Note Anonymous Types are internal, and by default Windows Phone (and Silverlight) does not allow reflection into internal types. To allow this anonymous type to provide data via binding, you need to add the following line to AssemblyInfo.cs:

```
[assembly: InternalsVisibleTo("System.Windows")]
```

Three important things are done in this sample: modeling our data using a database schema; creating a database and inserting data into it; and once the database is created, issuing queries and displaying the result in a UI.

Summary

In this chapter you saw how LINQ to SQL can act as an object relational model, mapping from objects and their associations to relational tables. You also learned the details of creating a DataContext to model the objects and creating queries that use joins to merge tables and where statements to filter results.

LINQ to SQL is instrumental in providing access to databases in every aspect of .NET programming, and is particularly important in Windows Phone programming where it is the framework for creating databases on top of isolated storage.

In this chapter, the powerful fundamental concepts of LINQ were applied to querying data from databases. In the next chapter, we'll see a similar flexibility with the Reactive Extensions. Instead of Rx in the world of .NET, Rx will be applied to the web, via the Reactive Extensions for JavaScript. The concepts from Rx translate exceptionally well to the asynchronous environment of the browser, and RxJS will enable elegant asynchronous code in the browser client, just as it does in the .NET world.

CHAPTER 7

Reactive Extensions for JavaScript

The concepts behind Reactive Extensions are universal in the world of computing; they are not specific to C# or .NET. To prove this, the Rx team at Microsoft ported the Reactive Extensions to JavaScript, and by doing so, brought the same powerful thinking about concurrency to the browser.

In this chapter, we will see how to take what you've already learned and apply it to HTML5 and JavaScript. We'll also see how we can integrate Rx with the popular jQuery library, and we'll learn how to take existing DOM APIs and events and integrate them with Rx. Using RxJS, we can replace complicated "spaghetti" code, consisting of many small callbacks and global state variables, with clean and succinct code that describes a complete scenario in a maintainable way.

Understanding JavaScript and C# Differences

When they are getting started with JavaScript, one mistake that .NET developers often make is to underestimate the ways it differs from C#. Even though JavaScript may superficially resemble C#, trying to treat it as such results in a lot of lost developer time and frustration. JavaScript has far more in common with languages such as Lisp or Ruby, than the statically-typed languages that we are more familiar with.

Spending some time properly learning JavaScript and its "Zen" will make a significant difference in your productivity. Douglas Crockford's *JavaScript: The Good Parts* (O'Reilly Media/Yahoo Press, 2008) is the classic reference for this perspective on the language, and will give you a thorough understanding of the quirks and "gotchas," as well as the interesting, elegant parts of the language.

RxJS Lives in a JavaScript Root Object

The Reactive Extensions for JavaScript (commonly abbreviated as RxJS) strikes a careful balance between being faithful to the .NET version of the library, as well as feeling natural and fitting into the conventions of modern JavaScript coding.

One of the first differences is that JavaScript libraries typically "namespace" themselves into a single root object, in order to avoid causing compatibility problems with other libraries. For example, all access to jQuery typically goes through the $ (dollar sign) object (as well as the 'jQuery' variable). These objects are attached to a "global object," which is a JavaScript concept—all functions and objects that are defined in a script file are implicitly attached to the 'window' object in the browser. RxJS namespaces everything under a single object, appropriately named "Rx."

To access Rx methods that would be defined as static methods in C# (such as `Observable.Return`), we must prepend the name 'Rx,' as in the following example:

```
var observable1 = Rx.Observable.Return(42);
var observable2 = Rx.Observable.Empty();
```

JavaScript Is a Dynamic Language

A fundamental element is missing from the example code we just looked at, one that would be required in the equivalent C# sample and that is types. How can we possibly have an `IObservable` without a type?

JavaScript is what is referred to as a *dynamic language*. This means that methods and properties of objects are determined at run-time instead of at compile time. Types *themselves* are mutable and can be changed! For developers who are used to static languages, this is a hard concept to wrap their brains around, but the end result is very powerful in the hands of a skilled JavaScript developer.

In RxJS, *every* `Observable` is essentially the equivalent of `IObservable<object>`. In .NET this would be very difficult to work with, but because JavaScript is a dynamic language, this is straightforward.

RxJS and .NET Method Names Are Sometimes Different

Because JavaScript does not support method overloading—i.e. a single method name that has multiple implementations based on its parameters, like `Console.WriteLine()`—some names of methods had to be changed in RxJS. In particular, the Window and Buffer methods in RxJS have names such as "WindowWithTime" or "BufferWithCount." If you can't find a method, check the Console to see if it has an alternate name.

Using a Browser Console to Explore RxJS

One of the best ways to explore RxJS is to use the Developer Tools built into most browsers. For Firefox, you should install an add-in called Firebug to get these tools, which typically include *a console window*. This allows you to simply type code in, one line at a time, and see the result—dynamic language programmers usually call this a REPL (from Lisp's "Read-Eval-Print Loop").

Some browsers also have useful features that make the Console easier to use, such as auto-completing method names, or allowing you to browse the contents of objects that are returned. One function that is particularly useful for playing with RxJS (though not compatible on all browsers), is `console.log()`, which is equivalent to .NET's `Console.WriteLine`.

Figure 7-1 shows the console window.

```
> observable = Rx.Observable.Return(5);
  ▶ Object
>
```

Figure 7-1. *The console window in action*

In the remaining sections of this chapter, we'll be testing all of our examples.

Jumping into RxJS

Let's take a look at how RxJS can be used in two simple examples. We'll use the same HTML page for these and other examples that appear in the first part of this chapter. For each demo, we'll modify the JavaScript script that executes. First, let's set up the HTML page and then observe how a simple `Observable.Return` and `Subscribe` works.

Libraries Included with RxJS

Since RxJS is a fairly large library and JavaScript developers are often concerned with the size of the code being sent to the browser, RxJS is split up into several pieces. Rx.js is the main library, and contains most of the operators and classes that are thought of as "Rx-proper." The Joins library ("When," "And," "Then") is split into its own file called `rx.joins.js`, and aggregate operators (i.e. "Aggregate," "Scan," "MinBy," "Sum," etc.) can be found in `rx.aggregates.js`. There are also a number of "bridges" included with RxJS that make using RxJS easier to use with popular open-source JavaScript libraries, such as Dojo or Prototype. Describing all of these libraries would be a lot to cover, but one bridge we will go into more detail with is the jQuery bridge.

Configuring an HTML Page for RxJS

The base HTML for our samples is fairly straightforward—just a `<head>` tag that includes the RxJS libraries we need as well as the jQuery library. The page also includes a `<p>` tag with an identifier that we can use later to replace its content. Take this code, put it into a file and name it `example1.html`.

```html
<html>
  <head>
    <script type="text/javascript" src="lib/jquery-1.6.2.js"></script>
    <script type="text/javascript" src="lib/rx.js"></script>
    <script type="text/javascript" src="lib/rx.aggregates.js"></script>
    <script type="text/javascript" src="lib/rx.joins.js"></script>
    <script type="text/javascript" src="lib/rx.jQuery.js"></script>
  </head>
  <body>
```

```
    <p id="content">Hello</p>
  </body>

  <script type="text/javascript" src="example1.js"></script>
</html>
```

Displaying the Contents of an Observable

For our first example, we will simply replace the Paragraph content with the contents of an Observable. To do this, we'll first create an Observable via `Rx.Observable.Create`, then Subscribe to it. Here's the code:

```
var simpleSubscription = Rx.Observable.Return(17);

simpleSubscription
    .Select(function(x) { return x.toString(); })
    .Subscribe(function(x) {
    $("#content").text("The value is " + x);
});
```

It actually looks similar to its C# equivalent if you squint a bit. Just like in .NET, the object returned by `Observable.Return` has all of the operators that we're used to having on IObservable. Here, we `Select()` a Number value into its String equivalent.

The `Subscribe` looks a bit different since the syntax to declare an anonymous function is via the 'function' keyword. In the subscription function, we use a jQuery selector to set the text of the Paragraph tag.

Displaying the Contents of a Chain of Observables

Using the same HTML page, we can do a more interesting example using several operators together, as follows:

```
Rx.Observable.Concat(
  Rx.Observable.Return(1),
  Rx.Observable.Return(2),
  Rx.Observable.Return(3),
  Rx.Observable.Return(4)
).Subscribe(function(x) {
  window.alert("Number " + x.toString());
});
```

In this case, we are using the `Concat` operator to take several `Observables` and connect them together, one after the other. The `Subscribe` function then displays a dialog on the screen.

Integrating RxJS with jQuery DOM Events

Let's see how we can take DOM events such as 'keyUp' or 'blur', and create an `Observable` based on them, similar to how we use `Observable.FromEvent` in .NET. The easiest way to do this is via the RxJS jQuery adapter (included with RxJS as the file, `rx.jQuery.js`), which is a jQuery plug-in that adds extra methods onto jQuery that make using RxJS alongside jQuery a snap!

RxJS adds a new method called `toObservable()`, which converts a DOM event to an `Observable`. The following is a simple example:

```
var keyDownEvent = $(window).toObservable("keydown");
```

The Type of the data provided by the `Observable` depends on the DOM event—for `keyDown`, the type is KeyboardEvent, which has a property called 'keyCode,' which we can use to get the key that was pressed.

Now let's look at a more complete example.

Example: Using jQuery DOM Events to Detect a Konami Code

People who grew up playing a lot of video games in the '80s and '90s will have fond memories of the Konami Code (see `http://en.wikipedia.org/wiki/Konami_Code`). This cheat code was found in many games written by Konami, and usually gave the player "extra lives" or some other bonus to the game.

Several web sites, such as Facebook and Marvel Comics, have added this code in at various times in their history as April Fools' Day pranks or for other events, enabling some often silly feature until the next page refresh.

Implementing the Konami Code Easter egg using pure JavaScript can be pretty daunting, but with RxJS, it's fairly easy to detect the Konami Code pattern in the event stream using the Buffer operator. The following is the HTML. Paste it into a file called `KonamiCode.html`:

```html
<html>
  <head>
    <script type="text/javascript" src="lib/jquery-1.6.2.js"></script>
    <script type="text/javascript" src="lib/rx.js"></script>
    <script type="text/javascript" src="lib/rx.jQuery.js"></script>
  </head>
  <body>
    <p id="content">Do you still remember the Konami code?</p>
    <p id="hint" style="display: none">Up Up Down Down Left Right Left Right b a Enter</p>
  </body>

  <script type="text/javascript" src="konamicode.js"></script>
</html>
```

One important part to notice here, is that we've got a 'hint' paragraph whose style is set to 'display: none,' which means that at startup, the text is invisible. Let's look at the code, as follows:

```javascript
// NB: These values work for a US keyboard, but they probably don't if you're
// using another keyboard layout. You might have to do some experimentation to
// find the right values.
var up = 38;
var down = 40;
var left = 37;
var right = 39;
var b = 66;
var a = 65;
var enter = 13;
```

```
var konamiCode = [up, up, down, down, left, right, left, right, b, a, enter];

var konamiCodeFound = $(window).toObservable("keydown")
  .Select(function(x) { return x.keyCode })
  .BufferWithCount(konamiCode.length, 1)
  .Select(function(sequence) {
    // We now have two arrays, our konamiCode array, and an array of the last 7
    // keys pressed - compare the two to see if they're equal (i.e. the last 7
    // keys pressed was the Konami code)
    for (var i = 0; i < konamiCode.length; i++) {
      if (sequence[i] !== konamiCode[i]) {
        return false;
      }
    }

    return true;
  });

konamiCodeFound
  .Where(function(x) { return (x === true); })
  .Take(1)
  .Timeout(10 * 1000)
  .Catch(Rx.Observable.Return(false))
  .Where(function(x) { return (x === false); })
  .Subscribe(function(foundInTime) {
    $("#hint").fadeIn("fast");
  });

konamiCodeFound
  .Subscribe(function(x) {
    if (x == true) {
      $("#content").text("CheatCode Found!");
    }
  });
```

There's a lot going on in this sample, so let's go through it piece by piece. Remember, our goal is that we want to first create an `Observable` based on the keyboard input, and then within that stream of key presses, detect a *pattern* (i.e. items in order). So first, we have to define the pattern, using a simple array, as follows:

```
var konamiCode = [up, up, down, down, left, right, left, right, b, a, enter];
```

Next, we're going to actually build an `Observable` to compare the last *n* items to the array. First, we'll Select the event into the raw keycodes, then we're going to use `Buffer` (in RxJS, "BufferWithCount") to keep track of the last 11 characters. Once we have that, detecting the Konami Code is a simple matter of comparing two arrays.

```
var konamiCodeFound = $(window).toObservable("keydown")
  .Select(function(x) { return x.keyCode })
  .BufferWithCount(konamiCode.length, 1)
  .Select(function(sequence) {
    // We now have two arrays, our konamiCode array, and an array of the last 7
    // keys pressed - compare the two to see if they're equal (i.e. the last 7
```

```
    // keys pressed was the Konami code)
    for (var i = 0; i < konamiCode.length; i++) {
      if (sequence[i] !== konamiCode[i]) {
        return false;
      }
    }

    return true;
});
```

The end result is an `Observable` that for every keystroke, returns either `true` when the last key of the Konami Code is pressed, or `false` if the sequence isn't the Konami Code.

Instead of immediately subscribing to it, we can actually reuse this `Observable` to implement another feature; if the user is having trouble entering the code, we can give them a hint.

```
konamiCodeFound
  .Where(function(x) { return (x === true); })
  .Take(1)
  .Timeout(10 * 1000)
  .Catch(Rx.Observable.Return(false))
  .Where(function(x) { return (x === false); })
  .Subscribe(function(foundInTime) {
    $("#hint").fadeIn("fast");
});
```

This code is a bit tricky. First, we filter so that we're only notified when we find the Konami Code for the first time. However, we add a ten-second `Timeout` onto this—remember, that this means that if the `Observable` doesn't terminate within ten seconds, it calls `OnError` with a `TimeoutException`. We then `Catch` that error and turn it into a False Boolean.

So, we now have an `Observable` that always returns one thing—either True if the user entered the code in time, or False if they were too slow. In this case, we only care if they were too slow, so we filter this using `Where`, then finally we `Subscribe` and animate the hint.

Whenever we *do* find the Konami Code, we want to show the "Congrats!" message. The following shows where we do this:

```
konamiCodeFound
  .Subscribe(function(x) {
    if (x == true) {
      $("#content").text("CheatCode Found!");
    }
});
```

In this section, we've seen how we can use Rx operators to manipulate Observable Sequences whose source is a browser event, as well as acting on the result to change the HTML content displayed. With this information, you already know enough to begin to integrate RxJS into web pages, but where RxJS becomes more powerful is when you can integrate browser event Observables along with other sources of information, such as information from AJAX calls or Geolocation requests. In the next section, we'll see how to integrate these sources into RxJS and use them together.

Adapting JavaScript APIs for RxJS

Just like in the world of .NET, APIs that are available to us in the browser aren't RxJS-aware by default. However, JavaScript actually has an advantage compared to .NET—every API that does something non-trivial like write to a file or send a network request is *asynchronous,* via a callback method.

We've already seen how to wrap asynchronous methods like this via the `FromCallbackPattern()` example, and in RxJS it's even easier. In the following, let's take a look at how we could wrap a new API, the HTML5 Geolocation API:

```
getCurrentPositionRx = function(opts) {
  opts = opts || {};
  var ret = new Rx.AsyncSubject();

  // Our callbacks will just OnNext the Subject, similar to how FromAsyncPattern
  // works.
  navigator.geolocation.getCurrentPosition(
    function(pos) { ret.OnNext([pos.coords.latitude, pos.coords.longitude]);
ret.OnCompleted(); },
    function(err) { ret.OnError(err.code); },
    opts);

  return ret;
};
```

This code looks very similar to the pattern we've seen before while exploring `FromAsyncPattern` in .NET. First, we create a new `AsyncSubject`, which works just like the .NET version. Next, we're going to call the `getCurrentPosition` API, and provide it two callbacks: a function that is called when the operation succeeds, and a function that is called when the operation fails with an error. Since there are quite a few situations where this operation can fail, such as when the user denies us access, or if the user is on a desktop machine without Wi-Fi, we need to handle errors effectively.

Example: Using RxJS with HTML 5 Geolocation and DOM Events

Let's take a look at a larger sample of how we can use our RxJS-enabled Geolocation function in any web page. First, let's create some HTML, as follows:

```
<html>
  <head>
    <script type="text/javascript" src="lib/jquery-1.6.2.js"></script>
    <script type="text/javascript" src="lib/rx.js"></script>
    <script type="text/javascript" src="lib/rx.jQuery.js"></script>
  </head>
  <body>
    <h2>Geolocation + RxJS sample</h2>
```

```
<form>
  <select id="mapOpts">
    <option class="typeopt" value="roadmap">Road Map</option>
    <option class="typeopt" value="satellite">Satellite</option>
    <option class="typeopt" value="terrain">Terrain</option>
    <option class="typeopt" value="hybrid">Hybrid</option>
  </select>
</form>
<p>
<img id="mapImage" />
</body>

<script type="text/javascript" src="locationMap.js"></script>
</html>
```

Here, we've created a simple drop-down combo box with different map types, as well as a placeholder image. We'll use the Geolocation API to look up the user's current location, then use the Google Static Maps API to display a map of the area. Let's take a look at the code, as follows:

```
//
// Create an Rx version of getCurrentPosition, which calls getCurrentPosition
// then returns an IObservable object.
//

getCurrentPositionRx = function(opts) {
  opts = opts || {};
  var ret = new Rx.AsyncSubject();

  // Our callbacks will just OnNext the Subject, similar to how FromAsyncPattern
  // works.
  navigator.geolocation.getCurrentPosition(
    function(pos) { ret.OnNext([pos.coords.latitude, pos.coords.longitude]);
ret.OnCompleted(); },
    function(err) { ret.OnError(err.code); },
    opts);

  return ret;
};

//
// Create an Observable that watches the Selection form element, and select out
// the value of the option selected (i.e. in the HTML, it's the 'value'
// attribute on each of the Option elements)
//

var mapChangeObservable = $("#mapOpts").toObservable("change")
  .Select(function(x) { return x.currentTarget; })
  .Select(function(x) { return x[x.options.selectedIndex].value })
  .StartWith("roadmap");

mapChangeObservable.Subscribe(function(x) { console.log(x); });
```

```
var currentMapUrl = mapChangeObservable.SelectMany(function(mapType) {

  // Get the current position - if it fails, we'll instead return a canned
  // default position, just like how you would do it in Rx.NET
  var mapPos = getCurrentPositionRx().Catch(
    Rx.Observable.Return([40.714728, -73.998672]));

  return mapPos.Select(function(pos) {
    console.log("map should change to " + mapType + " with position " + pos[0] + "," +
pos[1]);
    return [mapType, pos];
  });
})
  .Select(function(typeAndPos) {
    var mapType = typeAndPos[0];  var coords = typeAndPos[1];

    // Our selector will return the URL of the Google Static Maps image
    return "http://maps.googleapis.com/maps/api/staticmap?zoom=12&size=400x400&sensor=true"
      + "&maptype=" + mapType
      + "&center=" + coords[0] + "," + coords[1];
  });

currentMapUrl
  .Subscribe(function(x) {
    // Set the 'src' parameter of the mapImage element to our URL
    $("#mapImage").attr("src", x);
  });
```

We've already seen the first part of the code, where we create an Rx-compatible `getCurrentPosition`. Next, we want to create an `Observable` based on the drop-down.

```
//
// Create an Observable that watches the Selection form element, and select out
// the value of the option selected (i.e. in the HTML, it's the 'value'
// attribute on each of the Option elements)
//

var mapChangeObservable = $("#mapOpts").toObservable("change")
  .Select(function(x) { return x.currentTarget; })
  .Select(function(x) { return x[x.options.selectedIndex].value })
  .StartWith("roadmap");
```

The Static Map API has several enumeration values, which we encode into the tag in the 'value' attribute. First, we create an `Observable` that fires whenever the Option changes.

Unfortunately, the change event doesn't give us very intuitive values that allow us to easily get the selected item out—we need to use several Selector functions to finally extract out the current item, then grab the 'value' attribute.

Finally, we get to the interesting bit:

```
var currentMapUrl = mapChangeObservable.SelectMany(function(mapType) {

  // Get the current position - if it fails, we'll instead return a canned
  // default position, just like how you would do it in Rx.NET
  var mapPos = getCurrentPositionRx().Catch(
    Rx.Observable.Return([40.714728, -73.998672]));

  return mapPos.Select(function(pos) {
    return [mapType, pos];
  });
}).Select(function(typeAndPos) {
    var mapType = typeAndPos[0];  var coords = typeAndPos[1];

    // Our selector will return the URL of the Google Static Maps image
    return "http://maps.googleapis.com/maps/api/staticmap?zoom=12&size=400x400&sensor=true"
      + "&maptype=" + mapType
      + "&center=" + coords[0] + "," + coords[1];
});
```

Since we're chaining two async methods, we'll use the `SelectMany` operator to call `getCurrentPositionRx`. However, since this function is likely to fail, we'll use the Catch operator to return a default location. As one last trick, we want both the map type as well as the position. To do this, we'll `Select` into an array that gives us both items.

Next, we'll `Select` one more time in order to convert the map type and position into an image URL. The Google Static Maps API is essentially simply a URL with predefined query parameters. Most of the ones we are using are static, but we need to specify the center coordinates of the map and the map type. One thing to note is, we could've done everything in one `SelectMany`—however, one of the advantages of Rx is that we can separate our concurrent work into logical steps, just like we can (and should!) split our normal imperative code into simple, small steps.

Finally, now that we have an `Observable` of URLs that arrive every time the user changes the map drop-down (or on start up), we will `Subscribe` and update the Image tag.

```
currentMapUrl
  .Subscribe(function(x) {
    // Set the 'src' parameter of the mapImage element to our URL
    $("#mapImage").attr("src", x);
  });
```

Using jQuery AJAX with RxJS

One use case that is particularly compelling for RxJS is its integration with jQuery's AJAX library. Dealing with multiple callbacks in JavaScript can be a particularly daunting affair, especially because in JavaScript it is much harder to track down errors due to the dynamic nature of the language. Fortunately, using RxJS to make AJAX calls is quite straightforward. Let's look at the following example, a function to search through the Open Source projects hosted on GitHub:

```
var searchGitHub = function(term) {
  var params = {
    url: "http://github.com/api/v2/json/repos/search/" + encodeURI(term),
    data: 'json'
  };

  return $.ajaxAsObservable(params)
    .Select(function(x) { return x.data.repositories });
}
```

Here, we're setting up a Hash object containing our parameters—these are identical to the $.ajax()
parameters from jQuery, except that we didn't provide callbacks for the success and error cases.
$.ajaxAsObservable from the RxJS JavaScript bridge (rx.jQuery.js) will add these callbacks
automatically, and connect them to an AsyncSubject, just like the one we used in the Geolocation
example.

Let's put the ajaxAsObservable function to work. First, let's set up some HTML for a GitHub
Repository search page, as follows:

```
<html>
  <head>
    <script type="text/javascript" src="lib/jquery-1.6.2.js"></script>
    <script type="text/javascript" src="lib/rx.js"></script>
    <script type="text/javascript" src="lib/rx.aggregates.js"></script>
    <script type="text/javascript" src="lib/rx.joins.js"></script>
    <script type="text/javascript" src="lib/rx.jQuery.js"></script>
  </head>

  <body>
    <p>
      <form>
        <label for="searchInput">Search GitHub Repositories:</label>
        <input id="searchInput" />
      </form>
    </p>

    <ul id="content" />
  </body>

  <script type="text/javascript" src="githubSearch.js"></script>
</html>
```

Nothing surprising here. We've created a form with a simple input box and a prompt, and we've
created an unordered list <ul> to store the results of our search. Now, on to the JavaScript.

```
var searchGitHub = function(term) {
  var params = {
    url: "http://github.com/api/v2/json/repos/search/" + encodeURI(term),
    data: 'json'
  };
```

```
  return $.ajaxAsObservable(params)
    .Select(function(x) { return x.data.repositories });
}

var textBoxChanges = $('#searchInput')
  .toObservable('keyup')
  .Select(function(x) { return $('#searchInput').val(); })
  .Throttle(600)
  .Where(function(x) { return /^\s*$/.test(x) !== true; });

var searchResults = textBoxChanges
  .Select(function(x) { return searchGitHub(x); })
  .Switch();

searchResults.Subscribe(function(repos) {
  $('#content').empty();

  var count = 0;
  $.each(repos, function(x, value) {
    if (++count > 10) {
      return;
    }
    $('#content').append('<li><b>' + value.name + ':</b> - ' + value.description + '</li>');
  });
});
```

One thing to note about Rx is that since you are decoupled from events and callbacks being in a non-intuitive order, code can be written in a very logical order. In this case, we want to describe the workflow of this page. The user types text into a box, we execute a search, and display the results. Writing code in this fashion means that it will be more readable and maintainable to other developers in the future.

As mentioned before, we start with capturing the input from the text field, as follows:

```
var textBoxChanges = $('#searchInput')
  .toObservable('keyup')
  .Select(function(x) { return $('#searchInput').val(); })
  .Throttle(600)
  .Where(function(x) { return /^\s*$/.test(x) !== true; });
```

Here, we're again using the toObservable operator to convert a DOM Event into an Observable. The Select turns the keyUp event arguments into the current text in the search box.

One important thing here is that just like on the desktop, we don't want to issue an AJAX call per keystroke—to limit this, we're going to throttle to 600 ms. Changes that come in faster than this amount of time will be ignored. Text that is blank or consisting solely of white spaces should also be filtered out—the Where clause takes care of that via a Regular Expression. This Observable now is notifying only when a search should be performed, with the contents being the search text to be used. Now, on to the interesting part.

```
var searchResults = textBoxChanges
  .Select(function(x) { return searchGitHub(x); })
  .Switch();
```

In this code snippet, Select is called to fetch the search results. Why not SelectMany—this is an async call! Effectively, SelectMany is "Select and a way to merge the results." SelectMany uses Merge, which has the result of returning results as soon as they come in. One could also use Concat, which would guarantee that operations would return sequentially, one at a time.

However, in this case, we don't want the latest result that was *returned*, as Merge does; we want the result that corresponds to *the latest issued request*. Networks are strange and don't guarantee ordering. An early request could take a very long time to return, and then overwrite a later (correct) result. The effect to the user would be that the search results they are reading suddenly disappear and are replaced with an old query!

We want to issue requests as they come in, but "forget" about responses that correspond to old requests. The operator that handles this is Switch. Just like Merge and Concat, Switch handles an IObservable<IObservable<T>> and "flattens" it into an IObservable<T>.

```
searchResults.Subscribe(function(repos) {
  $('#content').empty();

  var count = 0;
  $.each(repos, function(x, value) {
    if (++count > 10) {
      return;
    }
    $('#content').append('<li><b>' + value.name + ':</b> - ' + value.description + '</li>');
  });
});
```

Here, some idiomatic jQuery is used in order to clear the unordered list <ul> tag and append list item <li> tags to it.

Summary

In this chapter, we've seen how existing knowledge of Rx maps very well to the domain-interactive rich web applications. Despite some small differences between the two languages, Rx behaves the same whether you're working in the statically typed world of C# or the dynamic world of JavaScript.

By using RxJS, we can combine DOM events, AJAX network queries, and HTML5 APIs into a single language of async results. This is a very powerful abstraction, because we've removed the impedance mismatch between these three concepts. It is then possible to use them all together in an elegant way to write rich, compelling web applications.

In the next chapter, we'll change our focus from the web to the world of desktop user interfaces and learn about ReactiveUI, an open-source library that demonstrates how closely Rx can be integrated with the world of XAML (WPF, Silverlight, and Windows Phone), in order to write user interfaces using elegant, declarative code to describe how UI elements are related to each other. ReactiveUI is also a great example of how Rx can be applied to a particular problem domain.

CHAPTER 8

ReactiveUI

It would be easy to think of Rx as an esoteric extension of LINQ that doesn't necessarily relate to anything in the real world. Nothing could be further from the truth. Not only is Rx highly useful "out of the box" in many circumstances, such as simplifying asynchronous programming, but it is highly extensible and can be applied to specific problem domains.

The code interacting with the user interfaces that we've presented in this book hasn't been very elegant. In simple XAML-based samples, there is a lot of usage of `Observable.FromEvent`, as well as explicitly setting properties on controls.

While this approach is reasonable (though, again, not very elegant!) for small samples, it has a number of flaws. One of the most significant flaws of this approach is that it makes testing your application difficult—creating UI controls and simulating input is slow and unreliable. Another disadvantage is that it tends to result in code that is too tightly coupled and brittle. Instead, many applications employ a design pattern called the Model-View-ViewModel (MVVM).

The library combines the MVVM pattern with Rx, which makes managing concurrency and expressing complicated interactions between objects possible in a declarative, functional way. In other words, ReactiveUI allows us to describe how properties are related, even if the relation involves an asynchronous method call.

The Model-View-ViewModel Pattern

The Model-View-ViewModel pattern is a design pattern designed for XAML-based platforms and plays to the strengths of Data Binding (i.e. binding UI control properties to objects). In this case, the Model objects are the core objects that are used to represent application data, as well as business logic that is independent of a user interface. The View in our case is a UI control, such as a Window or UserControl, which actually implements the look of a user interface.

It's important to understand that there may be several views for the same data—for example, there might be a summary view that display statistics and an overview of the data, as well as a detail view that displays the details of a currently selected item. These two Views are displaying data from the same source, but in different ways.

The third part of the MVVM pattern is the most interesting one—the ViewModel. Put succinctly, the ViewModel is "a model of a View." What does that mean? Consider the example of the "New User" page on a web site—the View will have a "Username" field, a "Password" field, and a "Password Confirm" field where the user can retype their password. The User and Password fields fit great in the Model object, but the Password Confirm field really doesn't belong in the Model, as it's not really part of the *data*; this field is only used in this *View*.

In traditional XAML programming, developers are encouraged to use the Codebehind of the View to store the Password Confirm field—however, when this is done, we run into the same problems with testability and tight coupling.

How do we test the specification of "The OK Button can only be pressed if the Password and Password Confirm fields match"? We put this field into a separate object called a ViewModel. This ViewModel is a simple class (i.e. not derived from a UI control) where we can describe the *interaction logic* of our View. In our example, the code for verifying the passwords matched, as well as the code that executes when the OK button is pressed would be in the ViewModel object. For every (non-trivial) View, there will be a corresponding ViewModel object.

The Philosophy of the ViewModel

One of the powerful aspects of MVVM is that the goal is separate from *what* a command or property is, except for how it is invoked or used. ViewModels are "thinking" in terms of Properties and Commands. In traditional Codebehind-based user interface frameworks, the programmer is thinking in terms of Click events and control properties. When code is written this way, it means that the *implementation* of Copy is often tied to the event handler of the Copy toolbar button. Code that is written this way makes it very difficult to test, because instead of being able to test Copy directly, we must simulate the press of a button.

When writing MVVM ViewModels, it is critical to separate these two ideas and to define our commands (such as "Refresh," "Open," etc.). The View decides the way that these commands are invoked. Similarly, instead of storing our data in *SomeTextField.Text*, the data should go in a property that is bound to the UI via XAML binding.

What Every MVVM Framework Provides

There are quite a few open-source MVVM frameworks that exist, each with their own strengths, but all of them provide a few basic primitives to enable the MVVM pattern. First, they provide a base class for ViewModel objects that notify when their properties have changed by implementing an interface called INotifyPropertyChanged. This interface is important, because it notifies the View that it needs to update its data bindings. Another feature that MVVM frameworks often provide is a system to handle Commanding—handling when the user issues commands such as "Copy," "Open," or "Cancel." This is often accomplished by creating an implementation of an interface called ICommand, which is built into several UI controls such as Buttons or Menu Items.

Unpacking the ReactiveUI Library

The ReactiveUI library is a framework that takes all of the traditional MVVM classes and removes a lot of the boilerplate code associated with integrating Rx with a user interface. The core idea of ReactiveUI is that it allows developers to convert Property Changes and Events into IObservables, and to take IObservables and convert them back into Properties.

Another core goal of ReactiveUI is to allow you to describe when a Command can execute in terms of the ViewModel's properties. While other frameworks let you do this as well, ReactiveUI automatically knows to update the result whenever any of the dependent properties change, instead of via polling or calling an "UpdateTheUI" method.

Core Classes

The following are core classes:

> `ReactiveObject:` A ViewModel object (an object that implements INotifyPropertyChanged). However, this object also provides an IObservable called "Changed" that allows other objects to subscribe to when properties on the object change. Using Rx's powerful operators, we will see how to recognize state changes that we are interested in.

> `ReactiveValidatedObject:` A derivative of `ReactiveObject` that is validated via DataAnnotations by implementing IDataErrorInfo, so that properties can be annotated with their restrictions and the UI will automatically reflect the errors.

> `ObservableAsPropertyHelper<T>:` A class that easily lets you convert an IObservable into a property that stores its latest value, as well as fires NotifyPropertyChanged when the property changes. With this class, we can derive a new property from an IObservable.

> `ReactiveCommand:` An implementation of ICommand that is also an IObservable whose OnNext is raised when Execute is executed. Its `CanExecute` can also be defined by an IObservable<bool>. We will see how this is a very powerful way to define when a Command can be invoked later.

> `ReactiveAsyncCommand:` A derivative of `ReactiveCommand` that encapsulates the common pattern of "Fire asynchronous command, then marshal result back onto dispatcher thread." It also allows you to set a maximum level of concurrency (i.e. "I only want three in-flight requests"). When the maximum is reached, `CanExecute` returns false.

Implementing ViewModels with ReactiveObject

Like any other MVVM framework, ReactiveUI has an object designed as a ViewModel class. This object is based on traditional ViewModel object implementations in other MVVM frameworks, such as MVVM Foundation or Caliburn Micro. The critical difference is that it is easy to subscribe to changes via the "Changed" IObservable. While this provides notifications for any property that has changed, clients are often only interested in one or two changed properties. Fortunately, there is an easy way to retrieve these properties—via the `WhenAny` extension method, as follows:

```
var newLoginVm = new NewUserLoginViewModel();

newLoginVm.WhenAny(x => x.User, x => x.Value)
    .Where(x => x.Name == "Bob")
    .Subscribe(x => MessageBox.Show("Bob is already a user!"));

IObservable<bool> passwordIsValid = newLoginVm.WhenAny(
    x => x.Password, x => x.PasswordConfirm,
    (pass, passConf) => (pass.Value == passConf.Value));
```

The syntax of `WhenAny` seems a little strange to many people at first, so let's walk through the second example. The first parameters to `WhenAny` are a list of properties specified via anonymous methods. In this case, the code is interested in whenever `Password` or `PasswordConfirm` changes. The last parameter is similar to how Zip works; it's an anonymous method that is called to combine the two values and return a result. When either of the two properties changes, this method is called to provide the result for the final IObservable (in this case, passwordIsValid).

One important thing to know about ReactiveObject is that properties must be declared using a special syntax because a simple auto-property will not notify ReactiveObject that changes have occurred. The only exception to this rule is for properties that are initialized in the constructor and never changed afterwards.

The following shows how to declare a read-write property in a ReactiveObject:

```
int _someProp;
public int SomeProp {
    get { return _someProp; }
    set { this.RaiseAndSetIfChanged(x => x.SomeProp, value);}
}
```

The traditional implementation, as follows, is a few lines longer:

```
int _someProp;
public int SomeProp {
    get { return _someProp; }
    set {
        if (_someProp == value)
            return;
        _someProp = value;
        RaisePropertyChanged("SomeProp");
    }
}
```

WhenAny completes the first part of ReactiveUI's core strength—it allows a developer to easily convert a property into an IObservable representing when that property changes. This feature is very powerful, as it is essentially a way to declaratively create state machines using Rx.

What does this mean? Instead of using Rx to describe a complex event from several simple events, Rx and ReactiveUI enable code to be notified when objects are in a certain state, even if that state involves many different objects or properties.

ReactiveCommand

ReactiveCommand is an ICommand implementation that is simultaneously a simple ICommand implementation and some extra bits that are pretty motivating. First, we can treat this as a non-Rx enabled ICommand, using the Create static method, as follows:

```
var cmd = ReactiveCommand.Create(x => true, x => Console.WriteLine(x));
cmd.CanExecute(null);
>> true

cmd.Execute("Hello");
>> "Hello"
```

Here's where it gets interesting—we can also provide IObservable as our CanExecute. For example, the following is a command that can only run when the mouse is up:

```
var mouseIsUp = Observable.Merge(
    Observable.FromEvent<MouseButtonEventArgs>(window, "MouseDown").Select(_ => false),
    Observable.FromEvent<MouseButtonEventArgs>(window, "MouseUp").Select(_ => true),
).StartWith(true);

var cmd = new ReactiveCommand(mouseIsUp);
cmd.Subscribe(x => Console.WriteLine(x));
```

While the previous example is useful to showcase the power of using an IObservable for `CanExecute`, a far more practical use of this is to combine this with `WhenAny`. Conceptually, it's often the case that commands can only be executed when certain properties are set or not set. For example, let's revisit our NewUserLoginViewModel and see how we can implement the Confirm's CanExecute.

```
IObservable<bool> passwordIsValid = newLoginVm.WhenAny(
    x => x.Password, x => x.PasswordConfirm,
    (pass, passConf) => (pass.Value == passConf.Value));

var confirmCommand = new ReactiveCommand(passwordIsValid)
```

Now when the View binds to the `confirmCommand` ICommand via a Button or Menu Item, it will appear grayed-out unless `Password` and `PasswordConfirm` are equal. Whenever either the `Password` or the `PasswordConfirm` properties change, `ReactiveCommand` will re-evaluate whether it should be enabled or not.

One thing that's important to notice here is that the command's `CanExecute` updates immediately, rather than relying on CommandManager.RequerySuggested. If you've ever had the problem in WPF or Silverlight where buttons don't re-enable themselves until you switch focus or click them, you've seen this bug. Using an IObservable means that the Commanding framework knows exactly when the state changes, and doesn't need to re-query every command object on the page.

`ReactiveCommand` itself can be observed, and it provides new items whenever `Execute` is called (the items being the parameter passed into the `Execute` call). This means, that Subscribe can act the same as the Execute Action, or we can actually get a fair bit cleverer. Take the following, for example:

```
var cmd = new ReactiveCommand();

cmd.Where(x => ((int)x) % 2 == 0)
    .Subscribe(x => Console.WriteLine("Even numbers like {0} are cool!", x));

cmd.Where(x => ((int)x) % 2 != 0)
    .Timestamps()
    .Subscribe(x =>
        Console.WriteLine("Odd numbers like {0} are cool, especially at {1}!", x.Value,
x.Timestamp));

cmd.Execute(2);
>>> "Even numbers like 2 are cool!"

cmd.Execute(5);
>>> "Odd numbers like 5 are even cooler, especially at (the current time)!"
```

Converting Observables to Properties via ObservableAsPropertyHelper

With the `WhenAny` method, it is straightforward to monitor properties of objects and make decisions based on them. Often though, we'd like to take this IObservable and set it to an "output property." Consider the example of a dialog that allows the user to choose a Color via a Red, Green, and Blue slider. Each slider would be modeled in the ViewModel object as an Integer whose value might go from 0.0 to 1.0. In order to display the result, we need to combine these three values into a XAML Color object. Whenever any of the properties change, we need to update the Color property to match.

Creating an IObservable<Color> via `WhenAny` is fairly straightforward, but once this exists, we need a way to store that value back into a property. ReactiveUI provides this via an object called `ObservableAsPropertyHelper`, which will store the latest value from an IObservable. First, we need to declare an "output property."

```
ObservableAsPropertyHelper<Color> _FinalColor;
public Color FinalColor {
    get { return _FinalColor.Value; }
}
```

Note that this property doesn't have a Setter—the value of the property will be determined by an IObservable instead of being set directly. In the ViewModel's constructor, we will now describe how to derive FinalColor from the value of Red, Green, and Blue, as follows:

```
IObservable<Color> color = this.WhenAny(x => x.Red, x => x.Green, x => x.Blue,
    (r,g,b) => new Color(r.Value, g.Value, b.Value);
_FinalColor = color.ToProperty(this, x => x.FinalColor);
```

This setup only needs to be done once, in the constructor. Now, whenever any of the Red, Green, or Blue properties are updated, the `FinalColor` property will update to reflect the latest values.

`ReactiveObject` and `ReactiveCommand` are the two core tools that are needed to build ViewModel objects. With these, we are now able to model a View using properties and commands, as well as describe how properties and commands are related to each other. We can take properties and convert them into IObservables to determine when interesting state changes happen, and describe the value of a property in terms of other properties (or in fact, in terms of any IObservable). In the next chapter, we'll see how these features allow us to write very testable ViewModel objects.

ReactiveUI also has several features that allow you to handle asynchronous methods elegantly in a user interface. Every non-trivial application will be doing operations that need to run on the background, and ReactiveUI makes running these and retrieving the results easily.

Handling Async Methods via ReactiveAsyncCommand

In XAML-based UIs, if your event handler does something that takes a lot of time, like reading a large file, you will quickly find that the UI turns black. This is because the framework cannot render the user interface because it is busy reading files or waiting on a network call. In fact, Silverlight solves this by preventing you from blocking the UI thread at all!

The solution is to run on a second thread, but that brings up the second tricky aspect: all XAML-based frameworks have thread affinity, which means that you can only access objects from the thread that created them. Thus, if at the end of your work you write `textbox.Text = results;` the result is an exception, because a thread other than the UI thread is attempting to access a UI control.

The traditional solution to this problem is to wrap the setting code in a call to
`Dispatcher.BeginInvoke`, which queues code to be run on the UI thread. In traditional code, you find
yourself using this pattern quite a bit, as follows:

```
void OnSomeUIEvent(object o, EventArgs e)
{
    var someData = this.SomePropertyICanOnlyGetOnTheUIThread;

    var t = new Task(() => {
        var result = DoSomethingInTheBackground(someData);

        Dispatcher.BeginInvoke(new Action(() => {
            this.UIPropertyThatWantsTheCalculation = result;
        }));
    }

    t.Start();
}
```

`ReactiveAsyncCommand` attempts to capture that pattern, and makes certain things easier. For
example, user interfaces often only want one async instance running at a time, and the Command
should be disabled while processing is still in progress. Another common thing that great user interfaces
do is display an indication that something is happening in the background, such as a spinning icon or a
"Working..." message.

Since `ReactiveAsyncCommand` derives from `ReactiveCommand`, it does everything its base class does—
you can use it in the same way and the `Execute` IObservable tells you when a command begins to run in
the background. What `ReactiveAsyncCommand` does that would be hard to do with `ReactiveCommand`
directly is that it has code built-in to automatically keep track of the number of actions running in the
background.

The following is a simple use of a Command, which will run a task in the background and only allow
one at a time (i.e. its `CanExecute` will return false until the action completes):

```
var cmd = new ReactiveAsyncCommand();

cmd.RegisterAsyncAction(i => {
    Thread.Sleep((int)i * 1000); // Pretend to do work
};

cmd.Execute(5 /*seconds*/);
cmd.CanExecute(5);  // False! We're still working on the first one.
```

The key methods to note in `ReactiveAsyncCommand` are the "Register" methods—this allows you to
register a sync method or async method (remember, one that returns IObservable), which will be
executed on a background thread and returns an IObservable representing the results that come back.
This IObservable usually maps to invocations of the Command. Every call to `Execute` results in a new
item being posted to the returned IObservable.

Modeling a Simple Scenario, from Start to Finish

Up until this point, we've only seen some small snippets of how the different pieces of ReactiveUI work.
Let's take a closer look at modeling an entire simple View and its associated ViewModel. This ViewModel

will illustrate how to perform the common task of associating a Button with a command that runs stubbed code in the background, and placing the result into a UI control.

In the following, let's take a look at the View—in this case, a WPF Window:

```
<Window x:Class="RxBlogTest.MainWindow"
        x:Name="Window" Height="350" Width="525">

    <Grid DataContext="{Binding ViewModel, ElementName=Window}">
        <StackPanel HorizontalAlignment="Center"  VerticalAlignment="Center">
            <TextBlock Text="{Binding DataFromTheInternet}" FontSize="18"/>

            <Button Content="Click me!" Command="{Binding GetDataFromTheInternet}"
                    CommandParameter="5" MinWidth="75" Margin="0,6,0,0"/>
        </StackPanel>
    </Grid>
</Window>
```

A few XAML-isms to note here. First, we are setting the `DataContext` parameter of the top-level Grid to our ViewModel object. This means, that when we use XAML data bindings, they will be relative to the ViewModel object instead of to the View, which saves us some typing, and encourages us to *only* bind to the ViewModel object. Next, we define a TextBlock and bind its content to the `DataFromTheInternet` property. Finally, we bind the Button's `Command` property to a command we've defined in the ViewModel, called `GetDataFromTheInternet`.

The following is the definition for the associated simple view model class:

```
using System;
using System.Threading;
using System.Windows;
using ReactiveUI;
using ReactiveUI.Xaml;

namespace RxBlogTest
{
    public partial class MainWindow : Window
    {
        public AppViewModel ViewModel { get; protected set; }
        public MainWindow()
        {
            ViewModel = new AppViewModel();
            InitializeComponent();
        }
    }

    public class AppViewModel : ReactiveObject
    {
        ObservableAsPropertyHelper<string> _DataFromTheInternet;
        public string DataFromTheInternet {
            get { return _DataFromTheInternet.Value; }
        }

        public ReactiveAsyncCommand GetDataFromTheInternet { get; protected set; }
    }
}
```

In our View, we create a simple property called ViewModel—since we will initialize this in the constructor before `InitializeComponent`, this can be a simple property. Next, we define the data that models the View—our ViewModel. We define an output property via `ObservableAsPropertyHelper` as well as a `ReactiveAsyncCommand`. It *must* be a property so that XAML can bind to it, but the setter is protected, since we will only initialize it in the constructor and never set it again.

Now comes the interesting part—the constructor. Since ReactiveUI focuses on defining declaratively how properties and commands are related to each other, most of the interesting code in a ReactiveUI ViewModel will be in the constructor—you can think of this code as "wiring up" the properties to each other. This approach has the advantage that all of your interaction code is in one place, rather than hidden behind event handlers or callbacks. For many ViewModels, the *only* code will be in the constructor!

```
public AppViewModel()
{
        GetDataFromTheInternet = new ReactiveAsyncCommand();

        //
        // This function will return a "stream" of results, one per invocation
        // of the Command
        //

        var futureData = GetDataFromTheInternet.RegisterAsyncFunction(i => {
            Thread.Sleep(5 * 1000); // This is a pretend async query
            return String.Format("The Future will be {0}x as awesome!", i);
        });

        _DataFromTheInternet = futureData.ToProperty(this, x => x.DataFromTheInternet);
}
```

The end result is that for every time the user hits the Button, the `Execute` method of the command is called, which produces a value on the `futureData` Observable after five seconds.

Notice what was *not* necessary to do here. The code didn't have to use any sort of explicit async mechanism like a Task or a new Thread, and it didn't have to marshal data back to the UI thread using `Dispatcher.BeginInvoke` and the code reads way more like a simple, single-threaded application, again instead of chaining async invocations. Furthermore, there's something else that's very motivating: *testability*.

Using `Dispatcher.BeginInvoke` means that we're assuming that a Dispatcher exists and works. If you're in a unit test runner, *this isn't true*. ReactiveUI automatically detects whether you are in a test runner and changes its default IScheduler to not use the Dispatcher.

With `ReactiveAsyncCommand`, code can be running in the background while the UI stays responsive. However, some long-running operations, such as web requests, don't need to be repeated more than once—instead, this information can be cached, so that unique requests only have to be requested once.

Memorizing and Caching in ReactiveUI

One thing that is useful in any kind of programming is having a look-up table so that you don't have to spend expensive calls to fetch the same data that you just had recently, since fetching the data and passing it around via parameters often gets ugly.

A better way is to use a cache; that is, to store values we've fetched recently and reuse them. A naive approach would be to store the data off in a simple Dictionary. This might work for a while, but you soon realize, as Raymond Chen, Microsoft's principal software design engineer, says, "Every cache has a cache policy, whether you know it or not."

In the case of a Dictionary, the policy is unbounded—an unbounded cache is a synonym for "memory leak," since items are never removed from the cache, only added.

To this end, one of the things that is included with ReactiveUI is a class called MemorizingMRUCache. As its name implies, it is a *most recently used* cache—it throws away items whose keys haven't been requested in a while by keeping a fixed limit of items in the cache.

■ **Note** A dictionary is a memory leak in the sense that the typical (naive?) use of a dictionary is to test whether your object is in the dictionary, and if not, to add it. Since the contents of the dictionary are never purged and theoretically the dictionary lives forever, it will eventually consume all your memory—as well as all your possessions and your entire family.

Using MemorizingMRUCache

A MemorizingMRUCache is just a proxy for a function; when you call Get, it's going to invoke the function you provided in the constructor. One thing that's important to understand with this class is that your function must be a function *in the mathematical sense*—as in the return value for a given parameter must *always* be identical.

Another thing to remember is that this class is not implicitly thread-safe—unlike QueuedAsyncMRUCache, if you use it from multiple threads, you have to protect it via a lock just like a Dictionary or a List. The following is a motivating sample:

```
// Here, we're giving it our "calculate" function - the 'ctx' variable is
// just an optional parameter that you can pass on a call to Get.
var cache = new MemorizingMRUCache<int, int>((x, ctx) => {
    Thread.Sleep(5*1000);    // Pretend this calculation isn't cheap
    return x * 100;
}, 20 /*items to remember*/);

// First invocation, it'll take 5 seconds
cache.Get(10);
>>> 1000

// This returns instantly
cache.Get(10);
>>> 1000

// This takes 5 seconds too
cache.Get(15);
>>> 1500
```

Maintaining an On-disk Cache

MemorizingMRUCache also has a feature that comes in handy in certain scenarios. For example, when a memorized value is evicted from the cache, because it hasn't been used in a while, you can have a function executed with that value. This means that MemorizingMRUCache can be used to maintain on-disk caches—your Key could be a web site URL, and the Value will be a path to the temporary file. Your OnRelease function will delete the file on the disk since it's no longer in-use.

The following are some other useful functions:

- *TryGet*: Attempt to fetch a value from the cache only

- *Invalidate*: Forget a cached key on calling its release function

- *InvalidateAll*: Forget all the cached keys and start from scratch

Caching Results Asynchronously

ObservableAsyncMRUCache is the async version of MemorizingMRUCache, a thread-safe, asynchronous MemorizingMRUCache. As we saw above, MemorizingMRUCache is great for certain scenarios where we want to cache results of expensive calculations, but one disadvantage is that it is fundamentally a single-threaded data structure; accessing it from multiple threads, or trying to cache the results of several in-flight web requests at the same time would result in corruption.

ObservableAsyncMRUCache solves all of these issues, and provides a new method called `AsyncGet`, which returns an IObservable. This IObservable will fire exactly once, when the async command returns.

For example, imagine you are writing a Twitter client, and you need to fetch the profile icon for each message—a naive `foreach` loop would be really slow, and even if you happened to write it in an asynchronous fashion, you would *still* end up fetching the same image potentially many times!

ObservableAsyncMRUCache also solves a tricky problem. Let's revisit the previous example. As we walk the list of messages, we will asynchronously issue WebRequests. Imagine a message list where every message is from the same user. For the first item, we'll issue the WebRequest since the cache is empty. Then, we'll go to the second item—since the first request probably hasn't completed, we'll issue the same request again. If you had 50 messages and the main thread was fast enough, you could end up with 50 WebRequests for the same file!

When the second call to `AsyncGet` occurs, we need to check the cache, but we also need to check the list of outstanding requests. Really, for every possible input, you can think of it being in one of three states: either in-cache, in-flight, or brand new. ObservableAsyncMRUCache ensures that all three cases are handled correctly, in a thread-safe manner. Since `AsyncGet` is an async method, it works great alongside `ReactiveAsyncCommand`—use it as a parameter to the `RegisterAsyncObservable` method. The end result is a Command that fetches data in the background, automatically making sure to issue the minimum amount of needed requests, limiting concurrency, and caching repeated requests.

In the next section, we'll see how to wire this up by caching a web service call in Silverlight. The procedure will be very similar for other XAML-based UI frameworks.

Calling Web Services in XAML Using ReactiveUI

Remember from the previous sections that an IObservable can be used as a future, a "box" that will eventually contain the result of a web service call or other asynchronous function, or the error information. To this end, we'd really like our web service calls to all be vaguely of the following form:

```
IObservable<Something> CoolWebServiceCall(object Param1, object Param2 / *etc*/);
```

Recalling back to previous chapters, we're going to use the Observable.FromAsyncPattern in order to map a Begin/End pair of methods into an Rx async method.

An Important Note on Silverlight

Silverlight's web service generated client code does something a bit annoying—it hides away the BeginXXXX/EndXXXX calls, presumably to make the IntelliSense cleaner. However, they're not gone, the way you can get them back is by casting the MyCoolServiceClient object to its underlying interface (i.e. the LanguageServiceClient object has a generated ILanguageServiceClient interface that it implements).

Once we've got the function, turning it into a command is easy, via a new method introduced to ReactiveAsyncCommand—RegisterAsyncObservable. This method is almost identical to RegisterAsyncFunction, but instead of expecting a synchronous Func, which will be run on the TPL Task pool, it expects a Func that returns an IObservable as described earlier. The following is a simple example of a good ViewModel object that demonstrates this:

```
public class TranslateViewModel : ReactiveObject
{
    //
    // Input text
    //

    string _TextToTranslate;
    public string TextToTranslate {
        get { return _TextToTranslate; }
        set { this.RaiseAndSetIfChanged(x => x.TextToTranslate, value); }
    }

    //
    // The "output" property we bind to in the UI
    //

    ObservableAsPropertyHelper<string> _TranslatedText;
    public string TranslatedText {
        get { return _TranslatedText.Value; }
    }

    public ReactiveAsyncCommand DoTranslate { get; protected set; }
```

```
const string appId = "Get your own, buddy!";
public TranslateViewModel()
{
    var client = new LanguageServiceClient();
    var translateFunc = Observable.FromAsyncPattern<string,string,string,string,string>(
        client.BeginTranslate, client.EndTranslate);

    // Set up a cache that will call translateFunc
    var translateCache = new ObservableAsyncMRUCache<string, string>(
        text => translateFunc(appId, text, "en", "de"), 25 /*cached items*/));

    DoTranslate = new ReactiveAsyncCommand();

    var results = DoTranslate.RegisterObservableAsyncFunction(
        _ => translateCache.AsyncGet(TextToTranslate));

    // When new translations come in, "pipe" the result to TranslatedText
    _TranslatedText = results.ToProperty(this, x => x.TranslatedText);
}
}
```

Let's review what this fairly short and readable code example gets us. Using a few simple bindings, we'll have a fully non-blocking, responsive UI that correctly handles a lot of the edge cases associated with background operations. In particular, graying out the Button attached to the Command while the web call is running, saving off the results, then notifying the UI that there is something new to display so that it updates instantly, without any tricky callbacks or mutable state variables that have to be guarded by Lock statements to ensure multithreaded safety.

Example: Searching Asynchronously for Images with ReactiveUI

In this section, we'll create an application that searches the public Flickr database of images. The user will enter a term and when the user stops typing, we'll search for images that match the requested topics, as shown in Figure 8-1. This will exercise the ReactiveUI library and illustrate real-world usage of many of the techniques we've described.

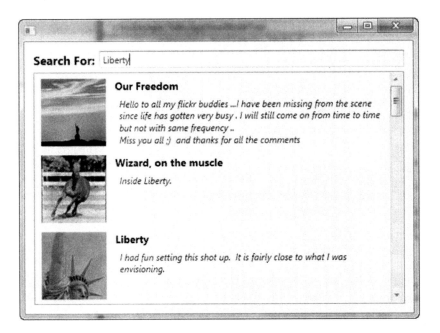

Figure 8-1. The completed project: searching Flickr

Design the App for MVVM

A key goal of the ReactiveUI library is to facilitate creating programs using the MVVM pattern. This program will create the following two classes:

- MainWindow (the view)
- AppViewModel (the ViewModel)

The first line of the program creates a property to access the AppViewModel from within the MainWindow class.

```
public partial class MainWindow : Window
{
    public AppViewModel ViewModel { get; protected set; }
```

This ViewModel is instantiated in the constructor of the MainWindow.

```
public MainWindow()
{
    ViewModel = new AppViewModel();
    InitializeComponent();
}
```

To keep the code simple, we'll define the AppViewModel in the same file as the MainWindow. AppViewModel is where we will describe the interaction of our application.

```
public class AppViewModel : ReactiveObject
{
```

In ReactiveUI, the syntax to declare a read-write property is a bit different from what you may be used to. The goal is to notify Observers (as well as WPF) that a property has changed. If we declared a normal property, we couldn't tell when it has changed.

```
string _SearchTerm;
public string SearchTerm {
    get { return _SearchTerm; }
    set { this.RaiseAndSetIfChanged(x => x.SearchTerm, value); }
}
```

Next, we define `ExecuteSearch` as a `ReactiveAsyncCommand`—a command that manages a task running in the background.

```
public ReactiveAsyncCommand ExecuteSearch { get; protected set; }
```

Pipe IObservable to a Property

In ReactiveUI, we can take IObservables and "pipe" them to a Property—whenever the Observable yields a new value, we will notify `ReactiveObject` that the property has changed.

To do this, we have a class called `ObservableAsPropertyHelper`—this class subscribes to an Observable and stores a copy of the latest value. It also runs an action whenever the property changes, usually calling `ReactiveObject`'s `RaisePropertyChanged`.

```
ObservableAsPropertyHelper<List<FlickrPhoto>> _SearchResults;
public List<FlickrPhoto> SearchResults {
    get { return this._SearchResults.Value; }
}
```

Next we'll create a property to manage a spinner control to let the user know the application is busy when it is performing a search. We declare this property to be the result of an Observable, that is, its value is derived from another property.

```
ObservableAsPropertyHelper<Visibility> _SpinnerVisibility;
public Visibility SpinnerVisibility {
    get { return _SpinnerVisibility.Value; }
}
```

We're ready to create the constructor, which takes two optional parameters that are used in testing, as described in Chapter 9.

```
public AppViewModel(
    ReactiveAsyncCommand testExecuteSearchCommand = null,
    IObservable<List<FlickrPhoto>> testSearchResults = null)
{
    ExecuteSearch = testExecuteSearchCommand ?? new ReactiveAsyncCommand();
```

The Properties in this ViewModel are related to each other in different ways—with other frameworks, it is difficult to describe each relation succinctly; the code to implement "The UI spinner spins while the search is live" usually ends up spread out over several event handlers.

However, with RxUI we can describe how properties are related in a very organized and clear way. Let's describe the workflow of what the user does in this application, in the order they do it.

We're going to take a Property and turn it into an Observable—this Observable will yield a value every time the Search term changes (which in the XAML is connected to the TextBox).

We're going to use the Throttle operator to ignore changes that happen too quickly, since we don't want to issue a search for each key pressed! We then pull the Value of the change, then filter out changes that are identical, as well as strings that are empty.

Finally, we use RxUI's `InvokeCommand` operator, which takes the String and calls the `Execute` method on the `ExecuteSearch` Command, after making sure the Command can be executed via calling `CanExecute`.

```
this.ObservableForProperty(x => x.SearchTerm)
    .Throttle(TimeSpan.FromMilliseconds(800), RxApp.DeferredScheduler)
    .Select(x => x.Value)
    .DistinctUntilChanged()
    .Where(x => !String.IsNullOrWhiteSpace(x))
    .InvokeCommand(ExecuteSearch);
```

We would like the spinner to be visible only if a search is running. ReactiveUI lets us write this kind of statement in code.

`ExecuteSearch` has an IObservable<int> called `ItemsInFlight` that fires each time a new item starts or stops. We can tie that information to a visibility pattern (where zero equals collapsed, and greater than zero equates to visible). We then use ReactiveUI's `ToProperty` operator, which is a helper to create an `ObservableAsPropertyHelper` object.

The net result is that we've captured the idea that the value of `SpinnerVisibility` is the in-flight items.

```
_SpinnerVisibility = ExecuteSearch.ItemsInflight
    .Select(x => x > 0 ? Visibility.Visible :
        Visibility.Collapsed)
    .ToProperty(this, x => x.SpinnerVisibility,
        Visibility.Hidden);
```

Next, we'll describe what happens when the Command is invoked. We're going to run the `GetSearchResultsFromFlickr` method every time the Command is executed. Pay particular attention to the return value, an Observable. We'll end up with a stream of `FlickrPhoto` lists. Every time someone calls `Execute`, we end up with a new list.

```
IObservable<List<FlickrPhoto>> results;
if (testSearchResults != null) {
    results = testSearchResults;
} else {
    results =
        ExecuteSearch.RegisterAsyncFunction(
        term => GetSearchResultsFromFlickr((string)term));
}
```

We take each list and put it into the `SearchResults` property, as follows:

```
_SearchResults = results.ToProperty(
    this,
    x => x.SearchResults,
    new List<FlickrPhoto>());
```

Listing 8-1 shows the complete code listing, including the `GetSearchResultsFromFlickr` method that does the work of searching and returning lists of `FlickrPhotos`.

Listing 8-1. GetSearchResultsFromFlickr

```
using System;
using System.Collections.Generic;
using System.Globalization;
using System.Linq;
using System.Reactive.Linq;
using System.Text.RegularExpressions;
using System.Web;
using System.Windows;
using System.Xml.Linq;
using ReactiveUI;
using ReactiveUI.Xaml;

namespace RxUISample
{
    public partial class MainWindow : Window
    {
        public AppViewModel ViewModel { get; protected set; }
        public MainWindow()
        {
            ViewModel = new AppViewModel();
            InitializeComponent();
        }
    }

    public class FlickrPhoto
    {
        public string Title { get; set; }
        public string Description { get; set; }
        public string Url { get; set; }
    }

    public class AppViewModel : ReactiveObject
    {
        string _SearchTerm;
        public string SearchTerm {
            get { return _SearchTerm; }
            set { this.RaiseAndSetIfChanged(x => x.SearchTerm, value); }
        }

        public ReactiveAsyncCommand ExecuteSearch { get; protected set; }


        ObservableAsPropertyHelper<List<FlickrPhoto>> _SearchResults;
        public List<FlickrPhoto> SearchResults {
            get { return this._SearchResults.Value; }
        }
```

```
ObservableAsPropertyHelper<Visibility> _SpinnerVisibility;
public Visibility SpinnerVisibility {
    get { return _SpinnerVisibility.Value; }
}

public AppViewModel(
    ReactiveAsyncCommand testExecuteSearchCommand = null,
    IObservable<List<FlickrPhoto>> testSearchResults = null)
{
    ExecuteSearch = testExecuteSearchCommand ??
        new ReactiveAsyncCommand();

    this.ObservableForProperty(x => x.SearchTerm)
        .Throttle(TimeSpan.FromMilliseconds(800),
            RxApp.DeferredScheduler)
        .Select(x => x.Value)
        .DistinctUntilChanged()
        .Where(x => !String.IsNullOrWhiteSpace(x))
        .InvokeCommand(ExecuteSearch);

    _SpinnerVisibility = ExecuteSearch.ItemsInflight
        .Select(x => x > 0 ? Visibility.Visible :
                Visibility.Collapsed)
        .ToProperty(this, x => x.SpinnerVisibility,
            Visibility.Hidden);

    IObservable<List<FlickrPhoto>> results;
    if (testSearchResults != null) {
        results = testSearchResults;
    } else {
        results =
            ExecuteSearch.RegisterAsyncFunction(
            term => GetSearchResultsFromFlickr((string)term));
    }

    _SearchResults = results.ToProperty(
        this,
        x => x.SearchResults,
        new List<FlickrPhoto>());
}

public static List<FlickrPhoto>
    GetSearchResultsFromFlickr(string searchTerm)
{
    var doc =
     XDocument.Load(String.Format(CultureInfo.InvariantCulture,
        "http://api.flickr.com/services/feeds/photos_public.gne?
          tags={0}&format=rss_200",
        HttpUtility.UrlEncode(searchTerm)));
```

```
        if (doc.Root == null)
            return null;

        var titles = doc.Root.Descendants("{http://search.yahoo.com/mrss/}title")
            .Select(x => x.Value);

        var tagRegex = new Regex("<[^>]+>", RegexOptions.IgnoreCase);
        var descriptions =
doc.Root.Descendants("{http://search.yahoo.com/mrss/}description")
            .Select(x => tagRegex.Replace(HttpUtility.HtmlDecode(x.Value), ""));

        var items = titles.Zip(descriptions,
            (t, d) => new FlickrPhoto { Title = t, Description = d }).ToArray();

        var urls = doc.Root.Descendants("{http://search.yahoo.com/mrss/}thumbnail")
            .Select(x => x.Attributes("url").First().Value);

        var ret = items.Zip(urls, (item, url) => { item.Url = url; return item;
}).ToList();
        return ret;
    }
  }
}
```

Summary

In this chapter, we've seen how to use ReactiveUI, a library that takes the core principles of a technology (MVVM) and attempts to make them Rx-friendly. Since many parts of the .NET framework aren't designed with Rx in mind, a library to "bridge the gap" can enable code that is much cleaner. If you find yourself writing the same boilerplate code repeatedly, consider writing a bridge library like ReactiveUI. In this case, ReactiveUI enables writing code that is more straightforward, easier to test, and expresses code declaratively in an elegant way, as well as writing async UI code that works the first time and doesn't hang the UI.

While testability is mentioned as a significant benefit to Rx and ReactiveUI/MVVM in particular, this hasn't been demonstrated yet. In the next chapter, we'll explore Rx's testing features, especially in the context of ReactiveUI user interfaces. With Rx and ReactiveUI, we'll be able to simulate an entire user workflow, including asynchronous method calls, and deterministically write tests to ensure correct behavior.

CHAPTER 9

Testing With Rx

Rx itself is a powerful framework for testing. In this chapter, we'll see how easy it is to replace async methods with stubs and mocks that return predefined values. We can even make these canned values wait for a proscribed period of time before returning, making it far easier to test asynchronous processes.

We can even make stubs return with an error. This makes it easier for us to get code coverage over the error case.

Later in the chapter, we'll see how we can simulate the passing of time via `TestScheduler`, meaning that even though our tests appear to take time, they will run instantly and deterministically.

Mocking Async Methods

Developers typically find it difficult to test asynchronous and timing-related methods. Unlike synchronous methods, it's not enough for an asynchronous method to simply return a correct value; you must also mimic the latency of its response.

There are many tools to test synchronous methods, but testing their asynchronous cousins is tricky. Developers often use `Thread.Sleep()` to simulate a long-running method, but the method only influences the timing to a very rough approximation but still doesn't let you actually control the timing with any precision.

One of the core innovations of Rx is its orchestration of events over time. We've already used operators such as `Timeout`, `Delay`, and `Window`, to manipulate streams based on time. In this section, we'll see how easy it is to create a convincing async "stub," then we'll take it a step further.

If this is the signature of a method named `FetchWebPage()`...

```
IObservable<string> FetchWebpage(string url);
```

...then we can implement a stub for this method as follows:

```
IObservable<string> FetchWebpageStub(string url)
{
    // Check the URL and error out if the Url is invalid
    Uri testUrl;
    try {
        testUrl = new Uri(url);
    } catch (UriFormatException ex) {
        return Observable.Throw<string>(ex);
    }
```

```
    return Observable.Return(
        String.Format(@"<html><body><p>'{0}' not found</p></body></html>", testUrl));
}
```

We can use these techniques along with traditional test techniques, such as Inversion of Control, to replace all of the async methods with simple stubs, just as we could with normal sync methods.

Interfaces that have IObservable properties are also easy to mock, too. Because you control the stub class implementation of the interface, you can simulate different scenarios very easily, similarly to how smart use of IEnumerable in web applications allows you to simulate a database query result with a simple List<T>.

Testing Async Methods with .First()

For unit tests whose sole goal is to test the actual values coming out of a method, the easiest way to call async methods is by just adding .First() on the end so that it will wait for the result. The following shows how we could write a simple, value-based test for an Rx async method; we could even use this to test our stub to make sure it does what we want.

```
[TestMethod]
void FetchWebpageSuccessCase()
{
    var result = FetchWebpageStub("http://www.google.com").First();

    Assert.IsFalse(String.IsNullOrEmpty(result));
    Assert.IsTrue(result.ToLower().Contains("html"));
}
```

Simulating the Elapse of Time

Although the stub used in the previous example will return correct results, it still doesn't effectively simulate the passage of time. One way we can create a more convincing stub is by making it take time. One thing that is very important is that any method that doesn't return immediately should take an IScheduler parameter. We'll see why this is important later in this chapter, but the essential rule is, if you use any Operator that takes an optional IScheduler, make sure to pass it your custom one.

```
IObservable<string> FetchWebpageOnDialup(string url, IScheduler scheduler = null)
{
    // Fetch the result, but simulate a slow connection
    return FetchWebpageStub(url)
        .Delay(TimeSpan.FromSeconds(5.0), scheduler);
}
```

Or we can make it even worse, as follows:

```
IObservable<string> FetchWebpageOnAirportWifi(string url, IScheduler scheduler = null)
{
    // Just like Dialup, only it fails after making you wait
    return FetchWebpageOnDialup(url, scheduler)
        .SelectMany(_ => Observable.Throw<string>(new WebException()));
}
```

Using Virtual Schedulers

We've been using Virtual Schedulers throughout the book, but we've never explained how they work. Remember that anything that isn't calculated immediately in Rx is run through an `IScheduler` implementation—in other words, Rx never creates a `Task<T>` or calls a new `Thread()` directly, it always delegates to a `Scheduler` to do the actual work.

So, what if you created a `Scheduler` that didn't actually do anything, but instead just recorded the time that the scheduled item should run? Then later, you could say "Go!" and it would run each item in order.

Here's the powerful part: if you've got a record of the order in which items should run in, you can also say things like, "Execute up to 10 minutes in, then stop and let me take a look around." The `Scheduler` will then run down the list but stop once it runs out of items that were supposed to run from t=0 to t=10 min.

And here's where it gets even more awesome: since you know the order of the events in the timeline, you don't actually have to honor the actual times—just the order! You can run through all of the items as fast as possible, and you'll still get the same result, since you did everything in the same order as if you ran it in real-time.

Not only that, when you rely on virtual schedulers for tests, the results are 100 percent deterministic—unlike `Thread.Sleep()`, the same thing happens every time you run the test, no matter what.

As we hinted earlier in the chapter, the key to using Virtual Scheduler is to make sure every Operator that takes an `IScheduler` is provided your Virtual Scheduler. In complex programs, this might not be so straightforward. We can see one approach to solving this problem in ReactiveUI, to create a global Scheduler in a static variable that can be replaced in a unit test runner.

The following shows how we can test our `FetchWebpageOnDialup` method using `TestScheduler`, which derives from `VirtualTimeScheduler`.

```
[TestMethod]
void MakeSureFetchWebpageTakesTime()
{
    var sched = new TestScheduler();
    string result = null;

    var fixture = FetchWebpageOnDialup("http://www.yahoo.com", sched);

    // Save off the result when it comes in - don't use First() here or we'll
    // never make progress!
    fixture.Subscribe(x => result = x);

    // Fast forward three seconds in - remember, our dial-up simulation takes 5
    // seconds to return results, so we should still have nothing
    sched.AdvanceTo(TimeSpan.FromSeconds(3.0).Ticks);

    Assert.AreEqual(null, result);

    // Move to six seconds in, we should have results now!
    sched.AdvanceTo(TimeSpan.FromSeconds(6.0).Ticks);

    Assert.IsFalse(String.IsNullOrEmpty(result));
    Assert.IsTrue(result.ToLower().Contains("html"));
}
```

The Virtual Scheduler takes over scheduling; instead of actually executing the action specified by Schedule(), it instead builds a timeline internally of the order in which operations will execute.

Calling Run / Start actually causes it to run the scheduled items in order. This lets us have "TiVo for test cases" set some test methods to run. You can then fast-forward to the halfway point, test the interim results, and then resume testing.

Example: Testing a ReactiveUI Application with Rx

In this section we return to the extended sample, RxUISample, of the previous chapter, and we use Rx's testing library to help us write unit tests. Testing the interaction logic in a user interface is a great application of Rx's testing libraries because most non-trivial UIs run code in the background. Testing to make sure the UI responds appropriately is difficult to do. However, with Rx, we can model different user scenarios ("User clicks a button, types some text, and hits Search," for example), and make sure our code reacts appropriately. In the previous chapter, we demonstrated an application that searches for images via Flickr. Despite this interface being very simple, this application has a number of UI behaviors that we would want to verify: the search should occur when the text changes, the busy "spinner" should be displayed while the image search is in progress, it should be impossible to issue multiple searches at the same time, etc... Writing UIs that "feel right" is very complicated once you get into the details!

The three tests that we'll consider examine various assumptions about the workings of the AppViewModel. We'll place these tests in a second project (RxUISample.Tests) and within that, in a file named AppViewModelTest.cs.

Testing Throttling

The first test, SearchesShouldntRunOnEveryKeystroke, tests that the throttling is working properly and that we're only submitting the search when there is a sufficient pause. To do this, we need to provide the scheduler with text at various timing intervals. This is one of the great strengths of the ReactiveUI Test library.

```
(new TestScheduler()).With(sched => {
    var keyboardInput = sched.CreateColdObservable(
        sched.OnNextAt(10, "R"),
        sched.OnNextAt(20, "Ro"),
        sched.OnNextAt(30, "Robo"),
        sched.OnNextAt(40, "Robot"),
        sched.OnNextAt(2000, "Hat"));
```

In the first line of the test, we simulate the entering of text by a user, and we time precisely when each letter will is typed (the numbers shown are milliseconds).

Notice the first line.

Remember that in ReactiveUI, there are two Schedulers that the framework uses: the Deferred Scheduler (i.e. the 'UI thread'), and the Task Pool Scheduler (i.e. 'run stuff on the background').

Here, we create a new Test Scheduler, and call the With method —this means that inside the Action given, the "official" schedulers are replaced with our test scheduler. Once the block finishes, the original Schedulers will be replaced, which makes sure that our test doesn't affect the execution of other tests.

The next section of the text makes sure that the command can execute, but we stub out the actual search.

```
// Make sure that the command can always execute if asked, stub
// out the actual search code
var fixture = new AppViewModel(
    new ReactiveAsyncCommand(null, 1000),
    Observable.Never<List<FlickrPhoto>>());

// Wire up the keyboard input
keyboardInput.Subscribe(x => fixture.SearchTerm = x);

// Keep count of how many times the command was invoked
int numTimesCommandInvoked = 0;
fixture.ExecuteSearch.Subscribe(x => numTimesCommandInvoked++);
```

The test then "travels through time" to examine how many times the command is invoked. To do this, we use the test method RunToMilliseconds, which takes an integer and causes the test to execute as if that much time has passed.

```
sched.RunToMilliseconds(25);
Assert.AreEqual(0, numTimesCommandInvoked);

sched.RunToMilliseconds(40);
Assert.AreEqual(0, numTimesCommandInvoked);

sched.RunToMilliseconds(1800);
Assert.AreEqual(1, numTimesCommandInvoked);

sched.RunToMilliseconds(2010);
Assert.AreEqual(1, numTimesCommandInvoked);

sched.RunToMilliseconds(5000);
Assert.AreEqual(2, numTimesCommandInvoked);
```

Testing for a Spinning Spinner

In the next test, we create a dummy Observable to mock the call to the web service. Here there is a great strength of Reactive Extensions: mocking tasks that take time, normally a very difficult challenge, is a snap!

```
[TestMethod]
public void SpinnerShouldSpinWhileAppIsSearching()
{
    (new TestScheduler()).With(sched => {
        var searchObservable = Observable.Return(createSampleResults())
            .Delay(TimeSpan.FromMilliseconds(5000), RxApp.TaskpoolScheduler);

        var command = new ReactiveAsyncCommand();
        command.RegisterAsyncObservable(x => searchObservable);

        var fixture = new AppViewModel(command, searchObservable);
```

```
            // The spinner should be hidden on startup
            Assert.AreNotEqual(Visibility.Visible, fixture.SpinnerVisibility);

            // Invoke the command
            fixture.ExecuteSearch.Execute("Robot");

            // Once we run the command, we should be showing the spinner
            sched.RunToMilliseconds(100);
            Assert.AreEqual(Visibility.Visible, fixture.SpinnerVisibility);

            // Fast forward to 6sec, the spinner should now be gone
            sched.RunToMilliseconds(6 * 1000);
            Assert.AreNotEqual(Visibility.Visible, fixture.SpinnerVisibility);
        });
}
```

Notice that in the test we can fast-forward through time, as follows:

```
            sched.RunToMilliseconds(6 * 1000);
```

This means that we don't have to wait for the six seconds to expire; we can jump forward and make sure that the spinner is no longer visible.

Changing Search Terms

The final test we'll examine checks that if the search term is changed, we get new search results. We start by creating the following dummy Observable to represent the query:

```
        var searchObservable = Observable.Return(createSampleResults())
                .Delay(TimeSpan.FromMilliseconds(5 * 1000), RxApp.TaskpoolScheduler);
```

We next create a dummy command to pass to the ViewModel that will return our Observable, as follows:

```
var command = new ReactiveAsyncCommand();
command.RegisterAsyncObservable(x => searchObservable);

var fixture = new AppViewModel(command, searchObservable);
Assert.IsTrue(fixture.SearchResults.Count == 0);

fixture.SearchTerm = "Foo";
```

We now perform a test ensuring that at two seconds we have no results, but at ten seconds we do have sample results, as follows:

```
sched.RunToMilliseconds(2 * 1000);
Assert.IsTrue(fixture.SearchResults.Count == 0);

var sampleData = createSampleResults();
sched.RunToMilliseconds(10 * 1000);
Assert.AreEqual(sampleData.Count, fixture.SearchResults.Count);
```

Here's the helper method that creates the sample results:

```
List<FlickrPhoto> createSampleResults()
{
    return new List<FlickrPhoto>() {
        new FlickrPhoto() {
            Description = "A sample image description",
            Title = "Sample Image",
            Url = "http://www.example.com/image.gif",
        },
    };
}
```

Before completing the test we need to ensure that the two sequences are actually identical.

```
foreach(var item in sampleData.Zip(
    fixture.SearchResults, (expected, actual) => new { expected, actual })) {
    Assert.AreEqual(item.expected.Title, item.actual.Title);
    Assert.AreEqual(item.expected.Description, item.actual.Description);
    Assert.AreEqual(item.expected.Url, item.actual.Url);
}
```

Testing is an important part of the software development process. Tests represent, in a machine-readable way, the behavior you intend the application to exhibit. Your tests are essentially the code version of your design specification.

Reactive Extensions enable writing specifications around asynchronous operations that are simply too difficult to model using traditional methods. With Rx, modeling the behavior of asynchronous operations is now straightforward and deterministic. The behavior of code written using Rx can be thoroughly verified, with the end result of extremely reliable code.

In this chapter, we've seen how we can create mock versions of the asynchronous methods we've written, which enables us to verify the behavior of methods under different conditions. In addition to being able to write mock methods that take time or fail, we also learned about Virtual Schedulers, which enable these tests to run quickly and simulate the passing of time. We also saw how to move step-by-step through a timeline and assert the application state at each intermediate step ("Run a command, wait 30 minutes, assert state, fast-forward to the end, assert state.").

For a more advanced example of using Virtual Schedulers, the ReactiveUI sample application that is included with the code demonstrates how to test a complex example involving the passage of time. The sample application models a Pomodoro Technique timer. The Pomodoro Technique is a personal time-management practice where an individual focuses on working for 25 minutes, then takes a break for 5 minutes. Writing normal unit tests for an application like this would mean that every test run would take hours! However, with VirtualScheduler, testing that this application behaves correctly is now possible.

Index